MOVING UP!
WOMEN and LEADERSHIP

MOVING UP!
MOVING UP!
MOVING UP!
WOMEN and LEADERSHIP

Lois Borland Hart

amacom
A DIVISION OF AMERICAN MANAGEMENT ASSOCIATIONS

Library of Congress Cataloging in Publication Data

Hart, Lois Borland.
  Moving up!

  Includes index.
  1. Leadership. 2. Decision-making. 3. Women—
United States. 4. Success. I. Title.
HM141.H34   301.15′53   79-54834
ISBN 0-8144-5570-0

First Printing

*To the participants of my leadership programs,
who inspired me to extend this knowledge to
other women interested in effective leadership.*

Preface

WOMEN CAN BE effective leaders! This was not what was impressed upon me as I grew up. How did I come to believe this? As a girl, leading others in the usual high school organizations, I was fascinated with how groups worked, why people behaved as they did, and what made some people realize their potential more than others. Then the emerging women's movement spurred me on to increase my understanding of human potential, organizational behavior, leadership, and women. I knew I wanted the professional opportunity to lead others, so I sought the academic credentials that would assure my access to these opportunities.

During the process of obtaining my doctorate from the University of Massachusetts, I decided to combine my primary interests for my dissertation. Thus I developed, implemented, and evaluated my first leadership program for women. Fifteen women near and around Amherst spent over 24 hours increasing their self-confidence, learning and practicing a variety of leadership skills, and wrestling with the implications of being a woman leader. The results of this initial program demonstrated that there is an interest in leadership programs for women, that these programs must be geared to some specific needs of women, and that women can be effective leaders.

Subsequent programs evolved. Women from all kinds of professions and organizations as well as college students and entry-level employees attended workshops and seminars. The content of the program expanded to include all seven dimensions of leadership found in this book and to discuss issues in leadership.

The program took on the name Athena, after the androgynous

Greek goddess who was venerated among the great divinities for her warriorlike qualities as well as for her prudent intelligence and gift for making peace. She was patron of architects and sculptors, as well as of spinners and weavers. She guarded over many industries, and thus was eminently the working woman.

Even though more and more Athena programs were offered throughout the United States and in Canada, it became clear that there were millions of women who could never attend them because they had neither the money nor the time, or because they were working at the lower levels of their organizations, and thus were ineligible for important management programs. Therefore, this book. It was written for the women who want to be effective leaders, and for the men who recognize their potential.

This book is not complete. It represents ideas and activities found to be successful in the leadership programs I was associated with, but there are many more. The road to effective leadership is never ending, but well worth the trip.

LOIS BORLAND HART

Contents

1

So you want to be a leader

ARE YOU A WOMAN WHO:
- —Has recently been promoted to a new position, yet feels overwhelmed by this new leadership role?
- —Is a volunteer responsible for chairing a committee, church group, or community organization?
- —Must work for economic reasons and wants to obtain a higher-level and better-paying position in an organization?
- —Is frustrated by the lack of useful college courses or training programs to help women improve their leadership skills?
- —Faces difficulties on the job because of sexism?
- —Is struggling to balance professional and family responsibilities?
- —Would like to be a more effective leader in her present position?
- —Needs specific answers to the unique problems of a woman interested in leadership?
- —Isn't sure of her interest in leadership positions?
- —Feels isolated as a female in a leadership role?
- —Would like to learn how to "take charge" of her life and explore her potential?

A Guide to Leadership

Such concerns are common among the ever increasing numbers of women entering the professional market. You are not alone in your search for sound, useful answers to the problems involved in assuming leadership positions, in struggling with everyday survival in these roles, and in moving up the organizational ladder. Scores of women are excited by new leadership opportunities, yet discouraged by the realities of the working world and sincerely in need of a practical guide.

Moving Up! Women and Leadership is for women on the move in all types of organizations and in all types of leadership positions. It is a practical guide to understanding and learning the concepts and skills involved in effective leadership. Leadership is a complex blend of behaviors, attitudes, and values; mastery of its concepts and skills requires a concentrated effort. This book, therefore, asks you to participate actively and to take responsibility for decisions that only you can make.

Throughout the book, you will be instructed to stop and reflect on questions, write out answers, assess skills, and practice new techniques. Obviously, such a book should not be read overnight, but over a period of time so you can have the chance to reflect on the ideas presented and to apply what you have learned. The time and effort you devote to this project will deepen your knowledge of and skills in effective leadership.

Use the book as a resource and guide. Although it does not have all the answers, it does give you a framework for determining your needs and planning a program to meet them. The framework used throughout the book is called *organizational leadership*—a system for describing the skills most commonly used by leaders in organizations. These are grouped into seven major categories: communications, human relations, supervision, counseling, management science, decision making, and planning. Within each category the skills are grouped according to five levels found in organizations: first-line supervisory, low-level supervisory, middle management, top management, and executive. (Chapter 2 fully describes organizational leadership, and the subsequent skill chapters use the system to guide you in assessing your strengths and needs.)

The book offers numerous resources, both within the chapters and in the resources sections. Be selective as you read. Review the resources presented and choose those most meaningful for you and your situation.

Moving Up! Women and Leadership is based on two assumptions. The first is that a leader does not learn and grow in isolation. Women moving into leadership need to seek support from others, using the socio-emotional, financial, psychological, and intellectual resources others can provide. (Many ideas on identifying and obtaining support are found in Chapter 10.) In the process of preparing for leadership you must not only receive but also give this support. Other women interested in moving into leadership need your help as you need theirs. The support must be reciprocal. Even as you are on the road to increasingly responsible leadership positions, reach out to other women who need your ideas, resources, and support. Too often, women who have "made it to the top" forget those behind them.

The second assumption is that *you* are in charge of your life. You have the power to decide what to do and how to take action. You are the final decision maker. Only you can determine your interest in pursuing leadership roles, the types of roles you'd like to play, the kind of life you want to lead. The book is a guide to facilitate your thinking, stimulate your aspirations, and offer resources. But in the end, *you decide.*

Realities of the Working World

In 1920, only 20 percent of all women 16 years and over were in the workforce. The percentage has risen steadily, reaching 43 percent in 1970 and nearly 50 percent today. Today women make up about 41 percent of the total workforce.[1] Think about your own family. In 1910, did your grandmother or great-grandmother work? How much of your mother's lifetime has been or was spent in the workforce? If you are black or from the working class, how was your mother's job viewed by the family? Recall when you first seriously considered that work might be a major part of your adult life. Did you think about it as you planned high school courses? Did you consider it when you found yourself single or newly unmarried because of death, separation, or divorce? Did it emerge as a need for economic survival?

The reality is that you, like increasing numbers of women, are planning to work throughout your adult life. You may be motivated by economic need, a desire for personal accomplishment and satisfaction, or a desire to contribute to society. Whatever your reason, you will probably spend a large portion of your life in the workforce.

However, consider the kinds of jobs you and other women have held. One-third of women entering the workforce start in bookkeeping, secretarial, typing, and clerical positions; 18 percent in factory and farm jobs; and 21 percent in service work, such as teaching, librarianships, and nursing. Such a narrow range of options limits women's opportunities to apply the full range of their potential. Worse still, most women remain in these entry-level jobs.

The facts about women moving into more responsible leadership positions are both good and bad. The number of women in professional, managerial, technical, and administrative positions increased from 4.4 million in 1965 to 7 million in 1975; and one out of six young women today plan for a career in business or a profession. Still, very few women are securing top management positions. Currently, only 1 percent of vice presidential or higher executive positions in U.S.

corporations and 6 percent of all middle management positions are held by women.[2]

According to the Council on Economic Priorities, a private research group, the proportion of women officials and managers at 24 large U.S. banks grew from 16 percent to 26 percent in five years, but the women's positions were predominantly entry level, in supervisory or management training.[3]

In education, a profession that has traditionally employed large numbers of women, the leaders of school districts are seldom female. High school principalships, once shared by women, have dropped from 10 percent in 1965 to 7 percent today, and elementary school principalships from 55 percent in 1928 to 20 percent today. Women superintendents make up less than 1 percent of the total.[4]

Yet women today are more educated than ever before in American history. They have the intelligence, interest, and determination needed to seek and hold responsible leadership positions. Although many still lack confidence in their abilities, more and more continue to build a foundation from which to spring into leadership. This book presents guidelines for the development of your individual springboard.

What is the reality of your working life? Assess it. How did you get into your current occupation? At what level did you start? How long have you stayed at each level? What opportunities are currently available to you to obtain supervisory and managerial positions in your occupation?

A Goal for Leadership

Think about leaders you have known, observed, or read about. What is your overall impression of them? How would you describe them generally? The most common answer to this question has been that leaders are "authoritarian, dictatorial, controlling, too uninvolved, or ineffective." How accurately does this statement describe your observations about leaders? It is because of these negative impressions of leaders that many women today are not so sure they want to be leaders; they do not want to model themselves after those they have seen or know about.

Although such a reluctance to emulate other leaders is understandable, leadership does not have to be this way for you. The following model presents a goal for leadership. The model defines effective leaders as those who are true to themselves, androgynous, and authentic.

Leaders must be true to themselves. To be "true to the self" means getting in touch with your personal values, beliefs, goals, and strengths.

Once identified, these characteristics and beliefs become the foundation for your plans and behaviors. A person's essence is maintained when she is true to herself.

Two problems emerge for women as they attempt to remain true to themselves. First, many of the characteristics that are more highly developed in women as a group—vulnerability, weakness, helpfulness, emotiveness, cooperation, participation in others' development, and creativity—are usually discounted or discarded as nonvaluable by the male-dominated world, and even by some women. Jean Baker Miller, in *Toward a New Psychology of Women,* presents a strong argument that these characteristics are, in fact, strengths—that they are essential to and form the basis for a more advanced form of living.[5] Assigning a positive value to these characteristics confounds all the messages women have previously received about themselves and encourages women to reorient their thinking.

The second problem women face in remaining true to themselves is that they often feel they must become more like men to be effective leaders—that they must, among other things, suppress emotion and be aggressive, tough, and hard-nosed. This is not only unnecessary but undesirable. Women need not sacrifice who and what they are to be effective leaders.[6] Instead, women must reaffirm their strengths and make a personal commitment to remain true to themselves as they move into leadership.

Leaders must be androgynous. No one would argue that the highly technological society in which we live has created innumerable economic and social problems, including the stress on people's personal lives that comes from the increased pace. Solutions to these problems are not simple.

Fortunately, our society has untapped resources in both its men and women. To fully utilize these human resources, we need to create a state or climate in which both men and women feel free to choose from the full range of human behaviors. To understand this concept of androgyny, look at the confining, rigid way our culture has described men and women.

Historically, the stereotypic characteristics of the male role (such as aggression, independence, objectivity, rationality, and self-control) have been more valued than those of the female role (such as emotiveness, subjectivity, passivity, talkativeness, and gentleness).[7] This differential evaluation has led to the definition of "healthy adult" as "healthy male," thus implying the unhealthiness or sickness of the female adult. The traditional focus on differences between males and females has obscured the overwhelming similarities and resulted in a false and unequal polarization.

Masculine and feminine characteristics are not antithetical. The concept of androgyny represents a synthesis of the two, offering the possibility of a wider repertoire of behaviors. Instead of taking an "either-or" or "good-bad" position, proponents of androgyny envision "individuals who are capable of behaving in integrative feminine *and* masculine ways, assertive and yielding, independent and dependent, expressive and instrumental."[8] Androgynous men and women more fully utilize their total range of characteristics. The development of androgynous leaders is not only desirable but necessary for today's world.

Leaders must be authentic. The search for authenticity, which seems to begin around the age of 35, is aptly described by Gail Sheehy as the Deadline Decade.[9] It is a time in adult development when people reevaluate their lives. The search for a personal truth requires careful examination, confrontation, and finally renewal or resolution of the issues raised. In this process, people question what is most important to their lives and compare their evaluation against the norms and expectations of society. Authenticity emerges when there is a congruence between a person's personal "truth" and her behavior. In addition, a leader who is authentic speaks and acts in a way that is believable. The words she says, the plans she makes, the decisions she enacts, and the direction she takes are compatible with her values and beliefs. There is no "credibility gap."

Today's world needs leaders who have remained true to themselves, developed both their feminine and masculine characteristics, and moved in the direction of authenticity.

Surviving in the World of Leadership

Women in leadership must find ways to survive in the face of the realities of the working world. Too often women leaders do not survive. Many are dead-ended in the wrong departments, some never move beyond entry-level supervisory positions, and others suffer the difficulties of being the "token" woman. Many are succumbing to physical ailments such as heart attacks and high blood pressure, which have been common among men holding responsible positions. Many are responding to the difficulties of surviving the world of work with depression and discouragement. Improving your chances of survival as a leader is possible, but it requires hard work, support, and careful planning.

How can women increase their ability to survive in a world dominated by men? The working world of men is akin to an "alien country," as so well described by Betty Harragan in *Games Mother Never Taught You.*[10] It is a culture that is unfamiliar to most women and that utilizes certain communication patterns, gestures, group affiliations, dress codes, game skills, values, and norms. To survive, women leaders must learn the organization's culture—that is, how it is set up and how it functions. This does not mean that women must assume the behaviors defined by that culture, but they must be aware of the organizational environment in order to work in or around it and to maximize their effectiveness.

The widely male-dominated world of work provides daily evidence of sexist attitudes and practices. The working woman can attest to examples of offensive, degrading, or exclusionary language; sexual harassment; discounting of women's ideas and contributions; and unrealistic expectations. Women must learn how to cope with these realities and work to change them.

Women also need to learn to cope with the problems that arise as they reach higher levels in the organization. As you advance as a leader, you will be increasingly in the numerical minority. There will be fewer women on whom to lean and with whom to share your perceptions. In addition, at the higher levels you will face the prospect of longer work hours, travel demands, increased stress, and the need for greater mobility. Leaders at these levels must juggle the demands of both their professional and personal lives in order to survive.

Finally, to be effective—and to survive—women need to develop and apply leadership skills appropriate to their position in the organization. The organizational leadership system presented in this book describes the skills needed by a leader at each of five organizational levels. Preparing for each rung in the ladder can prevent you from rising to a position for which you are incompetent. (This principle is developed more fully in Chapter 2.)

The above descriptions, while harsh, are accurate. Your reaction may be that you want nothing to do with such a world. Before you reject moving toward leadership, read the next section; it is designed to help you decide if leadership is for you. As Hennig and Jardim recognize in the closing section of *The Managerial Woman*, this is the first and most important decision a woman must make.[11]

Making the Decision

Before proceeding with any journey into leadership, you must ask yourself: "What do I want from life? How do I want to spend my work and personal time?" Any subsequent decisions you make about leadership depend on your response. Your assessment determines the course you take.

Lifetime goals

The following exercise will help you clarify what you want. In the appropriate column on chart **#1** list as many lifetime goals as you can in ten minutes. Do not analyze or judge the items at this time, just write them down. Next review your list and, for each goal, answer the following questions in the appropriate column:

1. How long have you wanted this goal (all your life, past five years, six months)?
2. Which of your values (health, family, money, accomplishment, independence, and so on) relate to the goal?
3. Which goals are related to work (W), personal life (P), or both (B)?
4. How much have you done in the past to accomplish each goal? Use this code to record your answer:
   A Already accomplished the goal.
   B Done a great deal toward the goal.
   C Done some work toward the goal.
   D Done nothing.
5. Which goals would you like to accomplish in the next six months? In the next five years?

Now rank the goals in their order of importance to you at this time. As you look over the completed chart, what patterns do you see? Do you see goals you've held for a while but have failed to act upon? Are there goals you began working toward but never quite reached? How many goals are related to your interest in leadership? Do your personal goals interrelate with your professional goals? How?

Select the goal most closely related to your desire to be an effective leader and write a goal statement. At this point in your planning, your statement can be quite general. Be specific enough, however, to include the role and the occupational field you would like. You may want to integrate several lifetime goals within this primary professional goal. For example:

—I would like to head a marketing division in the computer industry.
—I would like to be dean of a college in a large university system.
—I would like to start my own business.

What is important is that you identify and *write down* your goal. As you review it, ask yourself the following questions:

1 GOALS FOR MY LIFE

Goal	Time held	Values	Related to			Past accomplishment				Desirable in		Ranking
			W	P	B	A	B	C	D	6 mos.	5 yrs.	

—Is this goal something I really want? How much? How do I know
how much I want it?

—Is my goal specific enough to encourage planning and action, or
is it too general, too abstract?

—Is the goal realistic? Can it be accomplished? How much time is
needed to accomplish it?

—Is it a moderately challenging risk?

—How much room is there for personal responsibility in accomplishing it? How much is left to chance or other people? Can
others help me work on this goal?

—Is it a real goal, or is it a "front" for some other, hidden goal?

Keep your statement goal in mind as you continue reading. By the
end of the book you will have had the opportunity to clarify your goal
and to determine ways to reach it.

What price and rewards for leadership?

As you explore your interest in becoming a leader, you must
evaluate the risks and rewards it poses for you. Women tend to view
risk as negative or painful rather than as an opportunity for gain as well
as loss. (Risk taking is described in Chapter 10.) Any career that
provides the opportunity to develop leadership potential will demand
sacrifices, but it will also carry rewards. Buying a product costs money,
but you receive satisfaction from it.

Assess the price and rewards that moving into leadership holds for
you. Ask yourself:

—Do I really want to succeed in my career? How would my life
change if I succeeded?

—Am I willing to compete with men? Women?

—Am I willing to learn how organizations really operate and to
"play the game" by that system?

—Am I willing and able to arrange my personal life so that I can
attend to the demands of a career?

—Can I commit myself to developing and following through on an
action plan?

—Am I willing to be in the minority as I move into a "man's
world"?

Leadership rewards vary with the individual and with the situation.
If you pursue your goal, which rewards are you most likely to obtain?
Which do you value the most? Rank the items listed below in the order
of their value to you, from 1 for most valued to 10 for least valued. If

any other items are important to you, add and rank them. Next, check off those values you think would most likely be rewarded if you pursued your career goal.

	Values	*Rewards*
Friends	_____	_____
Independence	_____	_____
Financial Security	_____	_____
Mobility	_____	_____
Prestige	_____	_____
Achievement	_____	_____
Leisure Time	_____	_____
Self-fulfillment	_____	_____
Family	_____	_____
Service to Others	_____	_____

How closely related are the values you hold most dear to the rewards you would receive by pursuing your career goal? If they are closely related, your goal for leadership is probably well integrated into your life. If they are quite diverse, you need to reevaluate your values and your lifetime goals.

Now that you've thought about possible prices and rewards for a career in leadership, indicate on the scale below how certain you are that you want to reach your leadership goal:

1	2	3	4	5	6	7	8	9	10
I'm not interested				I'm still unsure					I'm certain

If you think leadership isn't for you, fine. Leadership is not for everyone. Find a role that suits *you*. If, however, you are still interested, read on. You are now ready to further clarify your goal. Add the following information to the goal statement you wrote earlier:

The date five years from now.
The kind of career you want to have by that time.
Where you hope to be living (if this is important).
The organizational level you hope to reach.

What do you know? What do you need to know?

Getting accurate information is essential to achieving your goal. Before you begin specific planning, you must determine what you already know and what else you need to know in order to start your journey.

Find out as much as you can about the leadership role you are seeking. What kind of knowledge is needed for this role? What leadership skills are most frequently used in this role? What kind of prior work experience is required? Who do you know in this field who could answer some of these questions? Are there any written materials that could give you this information? If you don't know someone in the field and can't find written materials, call a company with a position similar to the one you desire, ask for the person in that position, and request an interview. The tactic requires some self-assertion, but you will usually find that people are willing to talk about their work and to offer you additional leads.

Identify your previous experiences as a leader. Think about all the times you have assumed leadership roles. Organizations are giving increasing credit to nonpaid and volunteer work, but you will gain that credit only if you make others aware of what you have done. Dig back into your memory file and think of all the paid and nonpaid experiences you have had, including any leadership experiences in school and in the community. List and describe them in chart **#2.** Try to describe your responsibilities and the skills required for each job as fully as possible. Suppose, for example, that you were the editor of your college yearbook, supervising a staff of ten. Your list of responsibilities and skills might include the following:

Responsibilities	*Skills required*
Assign tasks to each member of the staff	Delegation
Review their work	Evaluation
Work with the adviser	Interpersonal relations

Next, assess your leadership skills. What skills do you already possess? What skills will you have to develop for the position you are seeking? Moving up requires that you know not only where you are going but also what you have—and need—to get there. Opportunities to assess your strengths and needs are provided throughout this book. At each point along the way, you will find questions, charts, and lists to help you determine the leadership skills you need to be effective.

The next chapter, on organizational leadership, provides an overview of the major dimensions of leadership and the leadership skills utilized at each level in an organization. Once you understand the

2   SUMMARY OF LEADERSHIP EXPERIENCES

Leadership position	Dates	Responsibilities	Skills required	Number of people supervised
Paid position				
Community				
School				
Other				

organizational leadership concept, you can move on to the chapters that examine specific skills. At the beginning of each skill chapter, you will be asked to review your strengths and needs relative to that leadership dimension. Your assessment will guide you toward obtaining your objective.

If you are interested in becoming an effective leader, move on. Read, reflect, explore, apply, question, and lead.

REFERENCES

1. Alan Pifer, *Women Working Toward a New Society* (New York: Carnegie Corporation, 1976).
2. "Women at the Top," *Training and Development,* May 1977, p. 39.
3. *National Now Times,* February 1978.
4. "Woman Principals Decline in Number," *Washington Post,* February 16, 1978.
5. Jean Baker Miller, *Toward a New Psychology of Women* (Boston: Beacon Press, 1976), p. 274.
6. Joyce Brothers, "The Woman as Boss," *Mainliner,* March 1974, pp. 32–35, 57.
7. Inge Broverman, Donald Broverman, and Frank Clarkson, "Sex-Role Stereotypes and Clinical Judgment of Mental Health," *Journal of Consulting and Clinical Psychology,* Vol. 34, No. 1 (1970), pp. 1–7.
8. Alexandra Kaplan and Joan Bean, *Beyond Sex-Role Stereotypes* (New York: Little, Brown, 1976), p. 2.
9. Gail Sheehy, *Passages: Predictable Crises of Adult Life* (New York: Bantam Books, 1977), p. 350.
10. Betty Harragan, *Games Mother Never Taught You* (New York: Rawson Publishers Associates, 1977), p. 23.
11. Margaret Hennig and Anne Jardim, *The Managerial Woman* (New York: Doubleday, 1977), p. 158.

RESOURCES

Career Planning
Bolles, Richard Nelson. *What Color Is Your Parachute? A Practical Manual for Job Hunters and Career Changers.* Berkeley, CA: Ten Speed Press, 1978.
Scholz, Nelle, Judith Prince, and Gordon Miller. *How to Decide: A Guide for Women.* New York: College Entrance Examination Board, 1975.

Survival
Harragan, Betty. *Games Mother Never Taught You: Corporate Gamesmanship for Woman.* New York: Rawson Publishers Associates, 1977.
Korda, Michael. *Power! How to Get It, How to Use It.* New York: Ballantine Books, 1975.
Miller, Jean Baker. "Why Women Fear Their Power." *Working Woman,* August 1977, pp. 32–36.

Mintzberg, Henry. "Power In and Around Your Organization." *Training,* October 1977, pp. 35–37.

Pogrebin, Letty Cottin. *Getting Yours: How to Make the System Work for the Working Woman.* New York: David McKay, 1975.

Pogrebin, Letty Cottin. *How to Make It in a Man's World.* New York: Doubleday, 1970.

Women and Leadership

Brothers, Joyce. "The Woman as Boss," *Mainliner,* March 1974, pp. 32–35.

Hart, Lois Borland. "Training Women to Become Effective Leaders: A Case Study." Unpublished doctoral dissertation, University of Massachusetts, Amherst, 1974.

Hennig, Margaret, and Anne Jardim. *The Managerial Woman.* New York: Doubleday, 1977.

Loring, Rosalind, and Theodora Wells. *Breakthrough: Women into Management.* New York: Van Nostrand, Reinhold, 1972.

Williams, Marcille Gray. *The New Executive Woman.* Radnor, PA: Chilton Book Company, 1977.

2

Leadership
in an organization

READING THIS BOOK is an indication of your interest in leadership. But what is leadership? How do you determine what leadership behaviors are appropriate to a position in an organization?

What Is Leadership?

Leadership is the process of influencing one or more people in a positive way so that the tasks determined by the goals and objectives of an organization are accomplished. The leadership role can be either assigned or assumed. It can occur in a small organization where everyone is known or in a complex bureaucracy where few people even in a department know each other.

In this book, the terms "leader" and "leadership" are used to describe the various behaviors and activities those in charge exhibit and undertake. The terms "supervisor," "manager," and "executive," which describe leaders who function at particular levels in an organization, are used less frequently, as they are limited to such levels and too narrow for the purposes of this book. The term "leader" is generic and has thus been adopted throughout.

Opposite is a list of traits often used to describe leaders. Read the list, decide which traits are the most important, and rank them accordingly. (Use 1 for most important, 2 for next most important, and so on.)

Numerous researchers have studied similar rankings in an effort to isolate the traits most important for effective leaders. They discovered, however, that the list of most valuable traits changed, depending on the

Traits	*Ranking*
Tact	_____
Honesty	_____
Ambition	_____
Listening skills	_____
Courage	_____
Sensitivity	_____
Energy	_____
Intelligence	_____
Sense of humor	_____

variables in the work setting. In one situation, the most valued traits were intelligence and energy; in another, they were sensitivity and listening skills. After many years of futile attempts to identify the best combination of traits for effective leadership, researchers abandoned this method.

Researchers next attempted to describe effective leadership in terms of certain behaviors rather than personality traits. This change in emphasis was significant in leadership theory, because it led researchers to study and classify leadership behaviors according to different levels in an organization. In other words, recognition was given to the fact that a leader cannot be isolated from the situation in which she functions.

The new focus on *situational leadership* (see Chapter 5) resulted in a plethora of descriptions of leader behaviors. What some researchers called "fraternization," others called "consideration for people," "interpersonal relationships," or "focus on people." Similarly, supervision was described as "controlling," "delegating power," "directing," and "supervising." Yet each set of terms denoted the same basic function.

Leaders interested in increasing their effectiveness can become overwhelmed by the variety of terms and misguided by authors who maintain that their idea is the one and only. In reality, of course, no single idea or concept holds "the answer." As new ideas about leadership come into vogue, usually only a few new points prove to be important. When management by objectives (MBO), for example, was initially presented, it was thought to be the panacea for all organizational and motivational problems. Although MBO proved effective in many ways, it certainly did not cure all ills; it worked well in certain situations with certain people in certain organizations. In other words, the effectiveness of a theory depends on many variables. You, as a leader, must select the ideas and methods most appropriate to your situation.

The Organizational Leadership Model

With so many theories of leadership on the market, it becomes especially important to find a way to describe effective leadership as it functions within organizations. The *organizational leadership* model describes in broad dimensions the tasks and behaviors of leaders at each level of any organization. The model utilizes the interaction between the position, the role, and the functions of a leader to identify behaviors important for the accomplishment of tasks inherent to that position.

The United States Army studied leadership and management and produced a series of monographs on the subject for the benefit of Army leaders. In one monograph, researchers Stephen Clement and Donna Ayres organized leadership tasks and behaviors into nine dimensions: communication, human relations, counseling, supervision, technical information, management science, decision making, planning, and ethics.[1] Clement and Ayres then classified these tasks and behaviors according to five levels within the organization. Below are the five levels and the parallel positions of military personnel:

Level in Organization	Officer's Position
First line	2nd lieutenant
	1st lieutenant
Low	Captain
	Major
Middle	Lieutenant colonel
	Colonel
Executive	General officers

As Betty Harragan points out in *Games Mother Never Taught You*, the military is the basis for the American organizational structure. This evidently is no secret to male managers, but it may come as a surprise to many women. As Harragan notes: "Regardless of how or why the military mentality overtook the corporate structure, it is absolutely critical for aspiring women to understand that this is the primary layout of the business game board."[2] Clement and Ayres' model can readily be adapted to a variety of organizations—profit and nonprofit, large and small. The following positions are found in organizations other than the military:

Level in Organization		Examples
Low-level or First-line Supervisory		
	Banking	Assistant manager
	Industry	Foreman
	Education	Coordinator, department chair, vice principal
	Government	Supervisors
	Business	Office manager
Middle Management	Banking	Branch manager
	Industry	Personnel manager, general manager
	Education	Building principal, dean of college
	Government	Branch or section chief
	Business	Store manager, regional manager
Top and Executive Management		
	Banking	Vice president, president
	Industry	Vice president, president, board chair
	Education	Central office positions, superintendent, president of college
	Government	Center, agency, or regional director
	Business	Owner of business, vice president, president, board chair

Determining the level of your leadership position

What is the level of your leadership position? Use the classification scheme above to evaluate your role in your own organization. You can also obtain an organizational chart outlining the positions of key people. If one does not exist, draw one up yourself. Tips on doing this can be found in Michael Korda's and Betty Harragan's books.[3] As you examine your organization's structure, keep in mind that smaller or newly formed organizations have fewer people to accomplish tasks. Thus responsibilities may overlap. For instance, the first-line and low-level supervisory functions may be merged into one.

Countering the "Peter–Pam Principle"

Knowing your leadership position is only the start. You also need to understand a phenomenon frequently found in organizations and commonly referred to as the "Peter Principle." Laurence J. Peter observed that "in a hierarchy, every employee tends to rise to his level of incompetence."[4] Although Peter excludes women by using the gendo-centric "his," it is assumed that women can also be caught in this web. For this reason, the concept has been expanded in this book to the "Peter–Pam Principle."

How does it work? Have you ever done an outstanding job and been rewarded with a position at a higher level? The promotion was probably based on your accomplishments *at the previous level.* But how carefully were your willingness and ability to assume the new responsibility assessed? If these were ignored, perhaps you found yourself functioning less effectively in the new position and feeling less competent than before. You and those who promoted you may have wondered what happened. What happened was the Peter–Pam Principle—you rose to your own level of incompetence.

The consequences of the Peter–Pam Principle are disastrous for an organization and for an individual's sense of accomplishment and job satisfaction. The organizational leadership model helps to counter the Peter–Pam phenomenon in several ways. First, it provides a total

Figure 1. Organizational leadership model.

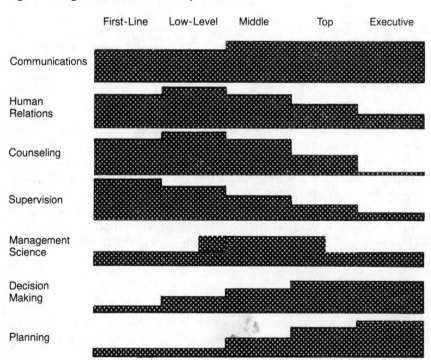

organizational perspective. It helps you see how your leadership position fits into the total organization and how the behaviors engaged in at your level are similar to and different from those at other levels.

Figure 1 provides a broad overview of the organizational leadership model that includes seven dimensions of leadership: communications, human relations, counseling, supervision, management science, decision making, and planning. The graph shows how leadership skills differ at various levels in an organizational hierarchy. The dark sections are equivalent to the amount of energy and attention a leader expends at each level for each of the seven leadership dimensions. As you can see, leaders at top management and executive level positions focus heavily on planning and decision making, while those functioning at supervisory levels focus heavily on supervision, counseling, and human relations.

The organizational leadership model also helps to counter the Peter–Pam Principle because it gives you the opportunity to assess the leadership skills you already have and the skills you need to move to a higher leadership level. With this perspective, you can prepare yourself for competency at a new level while continuing to use your current knowledge and skills.

The next seven chapters of this book are organized around the seven leadership dimensions. At the beginning of each chapter is a full description of the skills found in that dimension, how the skills differ by leadership levels, and implications for leaders. Then selected skills will be taught.

There are two cautions to keep in mind as you read about these leadership skills. First, no human behavior is so cut and dry that it can be classified neatly into categories. The leadership behaviors described in one chapter may be clearly related to those in another. For instance, conflict resolution is presented as part of human relations, but the skill is also important in management science, counseling, and communications. Further, skill in one leadership dimension often depends on skill in another. Thus personal counseling skills are directly dependent on the communication skills of listening and questioning.

Second, a common reaction when seeing all the leadership skills listed is amazement at the variety of skills involved in leadership. You may not only be amazed but also overwhelmed. While leadership is undoubtedly a complex process, keep in mind that you do not have to know or use all these skills *at the same time!* Actually, effective leadership occurs when the behaviors used are those demanded by the particular leadership position. Thus, you need to train yourself to focus on what is needed for each situation and draw upon and apply your strengths.

The choice is yours—are you ready to take this path toward effective leadership? Remember, the book is a resource for you to tap as it best fits your needs. You may choose to pursue only certain leadership dimensions or to carefully indulge in everything offered here. Keep in mind that the final chapter is planned to help you summarize your career goals, face the implications of moving into leadership, and develop a plan for action.

REFERENCES

1. Stephen D. Clement and Donna Ayres, "A Matrix of Organizational Leadership Dimensions," Leadership Monograph Series, No. 8 (Washington, D.C.: Department of Defense, Department of the Army, 1976). The organizational leadership model presented in this book is based on the work of Clement and Ayres, with a number of modifications in format and terminology.
2. Betty Harragan, *Games Mother Never Taught You* (New York: Rawson Publishers Associates, 1977), p. 20.
3. Michael Korda, *Power! How to Get It, How to Use It* (New York: Ballantine Books, 1975), pp. 107–115; Harragan, *Games*, pp. 25–33.
4. Laurence J. Peter and Raymond Hull, *The Peter Principle: Why Things Always Go Wrong* (New York: William Morrow, 1969).

3

Communicating up and down and all around

EFFECTIVE COMMUNICATION is a must for leaders at all organizational levels. Communication is at the core of each interpersonal experience; at the same time, it is often the major stumblingblock to meaningful interactions.

Achieving effective communication is especially complex because communication includes so many dimensions and demands intra-organizational and interorganizational skills. More specifically, as chart **#3** outlines, the leader must develop basic interpersonal skills of listening, speaking, writing, and reading in addition to organizational communication skills.

As you review the chart, notice that the skills required at each level differ. In interpersonal communication, for instance, the leader at the lower levels, who more frequently interacts on a one-to-one basis, needs skills appropriate to smaller groups of people. The leader at the middle and top management levels, who deals with larger groups of people, needs to develop speaking and listening skills appropriate to these groups. In organizational communication, the leader at the top who is responsible for determining policy needs skills for communicating within the organization, whereas the leader at the lower levels must know how to accurately communicate organizational policies and procedures to those whom she leads.

Assessing Your Communication Skills

In this and each of the other six chapters on leadership skills, you will be asked to assess your strengths and your needs for particular skills.

3 COMMUNICATION SKILLS

	First-line/Low	Middle	Top	Executive
Interpersonal				
Listening	• Listens empathically	• Listens for comprehension • Interviews prospective employees	• Attends meetings	• Listens attentively to reports of subordinates' viewpoints of others
Speaking	• Provides subordinates with feedback on performance	• Uses persuasion skills	• Attends meetings • Gives verbal reports and directions	• Gives organization's viewpoint to public • Gives directions to subordinates
Writing	• Provides daily production or service performance assessments to supervisor	• Writes reports	• Prepares reports and written directions to subordinates	
Reading	• Reads technical reports	• Reads literature sent by top level	• Reads reports on goals and performance • Reads current literature on own profession	• Reviews reports
Organizational				
Intraorganizational	• Disseminates information sent to this level	• Collects and passes on required information • Systematizes information • Develops informal networks	• Filters reports and data to executive levels • Develops informal networks • Recommends formal communication	• Sets policy • Determines formal communication system
Interorganizational		• Attends professional meetings as directed by executive office		• Meets with visitors • Serves as liaison with other organizations and government agencies • Attends conferences

Most people tend to negate or discount those abilities they have already developed; thus it is very important to complete both the positive *and* negative parts of this assessment.

In each assessment, you are asked to decide if you want to focus on improving skills used in your current leadership position or on developing skills for a higher leadership level toward which you are moving. Once you make this decision, reread chart **#3** to determine the skills you already possess at your chosen level. Rate the strengths of those skills with this code, writing a number next to each skill assessed:

+3   Highly developed
+2   Somewhat developed
+1   Minimally developed

For instance, if you listen to employees and colleagues in various settings and think you generally comprehend their meaning accurately, rate yourself +2 or +3.

Next, review the chart to identify those skills you'd like to develop more fully. Use a similar rating system:

−1   Needs minimal development
−2   Needs some development
−3   Needs considerable development

For example, if you notice that you are not fully aware of or do not use informal communication networks in your organization, you might rate yourself −2.

List the skills that need the most development on the planning sheet in chart **#4,** under the column marked "Skills I want to develop." Number those listed in the order in which you want to develop them.

What communication problems do women face? To begin with, they need to develop better mechanisms for coping with criticism, both received and given; they also need to develop the ability to speak persuasively so that they and their presentations are taken seriously. In addition, women need to consciously and regularly "read" an organization's communication systems, both formal and informal. This chapter addresses some of the patterns of differences in the way women and men communicate and presents several skills helpful to women leaders. More specifically, the chapter includes:

1. The communication cycle.
2. Listening attentively.
3. Clarifying messages.
4. Speaking out.

Skills I want to develop	Order of development	Found in chapter	Additional resources

5. Giving and receiving feedback.
6. Communication in the organization.

On your planning sheet, check any skill you've listed that is covered in the chapter. Use the space at the far right to list additional resources— either those listed at the end of the chapter or other resources you know about—that might help you in developing specific skills.

The Communication Cycle

What is involved in interpersonal communication? Why is effective, meaningful communication so difficult? Miscommunication is the cause of most interpersonal problems. Figure 2 identifies some of the key areas where problems can arise.

The communication cycle begins when one person wants to convey something to another. The sender has her own reason for sending the message and chooses a means to convey it; the receiver, in turn, internalizes the message, evaluates its meaning, and determines both a response and a means to convey it to the sender. The cycle is complete when the receiver sends her own signal.

Sally, for example, wants to review a procedure she has been developing with her supervisor, Mr. Vargas. He, however, arrives an hour late to work on the day she wants to talk with him. Immediately on

Figure 2. The communication cycle.

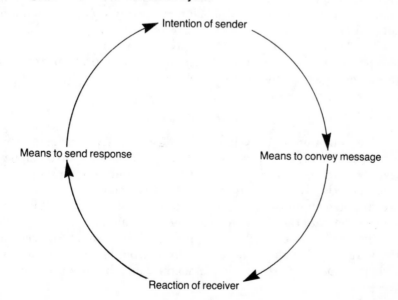

his arrival, she approaches him and asks, "Do you have any free time today?" (The message has been sent through verbal means.) As he internalizes her request, he is aware of his anxiety about being late, becomes defensive, and thus responds with "No, Sally, I don't! You will have to handle the matter yourself."

Miscommunication has occurred before the purpose of the question has even been raised. What happened? Although Sally was clear on her intentions, she failed to assess the situation before sending the message. In addition, both the sender and receiver perceived meanings in the other's verbal and nonverbal (such as facial expressions and tone of voice) messages that were not intended.

What could each person have done differently? Sally could have put more effort into determining the best time to present her idea to Mr. Vargas. She could have written him a memo requesting a meeting to discuss her proposal. She could have asked his secretary about the best time to schedule such a meeting. She could have outlined her idea on paper and sent it to him before making her request. When she realized that her request was ill timed, she could have changed tactics and said, "I realize this is not a good time to arrange a meeting, but I do have something important to talk to you about. Please call me so we can talk further."

Mr. Vargas, on the other hand, could have checked out Sally's intentions. He could have said, "I have to know more about what you need from me before I respond, but this isn't a good time. Please call me at ten o'clock and we can talk then." Instead, the encounter ended with a closed door, hurt feelings, and irritation. Sally and Mr. Vargas could have been more successful had they been aware of the communication cycle.

Problems can and will occur at any point in the cycle. Looking at each part more closely, you can determine your own problem areas and the communication skills that will help you most.

Intention of sender

The communication cycle starts most smoothly when the sender is very clear about the purpose and content of the message. Women have been socialized to deny many of their wants and needs; as a result, they often send cloudy or hesitant messages. Clarity about intentions short-circuits potential miscommunication. Stop and ask yourself, "What do I want to communicate?" Then *really* listen to your own answer. In the example, Sally was clear about her purpose: She wanted to meet with Mr. Vargas so that she could get feedback from him on her idea and perhaps gain support for implementing it. The problem in this instance, then, lay not in lack of clarity about the intention of the message but in the means chosen to convey it.

Means to convey the message

An effective communicator reviews the available means to convey a message and selects the most appropriate. The person who impulsively communicates, without consideration of the context in which the message will be conveyed or of the individuals involved, should not wonder at the resulting miscommunication. Sally's behavior demonstrates this.

What are some means of conveying messages? You can communicate verbally, in writing, or both. If you present your message verbally, you can begin with a statement or question; you can also use body language such as stance, gestures, and facial expressions to your advantage. If you write your message, you can prepare an outline and use graphics or other illustrative materials.

With these options, you need some criteria for determining the best means in any given circumstance. Ask yourself:

—Which means is most suited to the content of the message?
—Do you present yourself through one means better than another?
—Which means would most accurately deliver the message to this
  particular receiver?
—How much time is available? Is there time to write, or does the
  urgency of the message require a verbal presentation?

Reaction of receiver

Even if a sender is clear on her intentions and selects the most appropriate means to convey the message for that situation, the impact on the receiver still may not be the one expected. Messages are perceived, internalized, and evaluated within the context of a person's unique life experiences, needs, wants, and values. Thus the effect of any given message can differ from person to person. For example, count the number of triangles you see in the diagram below. Without

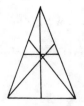

revealing your total, ask three other people to do the same. Then compare your scores. You will probably find that each person observed a different number of triangles. Each solved the problem with her or his own assumptions, knowledge, values, and needs. These differences do not make any one answer wrong or right, only different.

Another way to test differences in perception is to listen to an account of world news. Tell the news to a second person and then ask that person to convey the news to a third person as you listen. Ask the third to tell the news to a fourth, who in turn tells it to a fifth. Note how different the fifth version is from your original account. What happened?

All the participants were selective in what they "heard." This selectivity emerged from their own needs, values, and life experiences. They remembered and passed on details of the news that related to their own values, experiences, and needs and passed over details that were not meaningful or useful.

The point for leaders to recognize is that messages are interpreted according to the receiver's perceptions of the data. Even though intentions are clear and an appropriate means is used to send the message, it is the receiver who interprets the words. Knowing this, both the sender and the receiver can use the skill of clarifying (described later in this section) to check the accuracy of their perceptions.

The receiver's beliefs and attitudes toward the sender also contribute to how a message is interpreted. Stereotypic beliefs that women are or should be subordinate, inferior, and supportive naturally affect communication. Men (and women) who perceive women as subordinate will not seriously consider what women have to say. You may have had the experience of finding your ideas, questions, and presence ignored, slighted, or even ridiculed in a group of male colleagues. The receptivity of others toward your communication depends on their attitudes toward women in general. Thorough discussions of how to deal with this problem are found in several of the books listed at the end of the chapter. Check that section to find those books that might be most helpful to you.

Some of the key ideas include:

1. Believe in your right to your own ideas and your right to be heard.
2. Share your experiences with other women and develop ways to deal with the problem.
3. Draw attention to behaviors in others that contribute to miscommunication.

Means to send a response

After receiving and evaluating the message, the respondent must select a means to convey a response back to the sender. The criteria used by the sender to determine a means apply here as well. As pointed out in the example, Mr. Vargas could have responded in a way that opened up the channels of communication. Because of the circular nature of the communication cycle, in which the receiver, by responding, also becomes a sender and is instrumental in keeping the cycle moving, the choice made at this point is crucial.

As a leader, you have the responsibility to learn and practice communication skills that will enhance interpersonal relationships. The following sections on listening attentively, clarifying the message, speaking out, and giving and receiving feedback can help you meet that responsibility. Once you know these skills, you can share them with others through modeling or direct instruction.

Listening Attentively

Our need for the full attention of others starts at birth, yet the opportunity to gratify this need is limited by the ability of others to give us their attention. Think about your own need for attention. Scan the past week and recall when you had something to say at work or at home. What happened? Were you interrupted by the phone ringing or someone coming into the room? Did the person you were talking to redirect the attention her or his way? Did you have difficulty finding someone willing to give you attention?

Lack of attention from important people—parents, teachers, neighbors, friends, spouses, children, colleagues, bosses—leads to an unconscious craving for that attention. This need is expressed in many ways. Some people are excessive talkers, locked into dominating verbal communication, afraid to let go of the focus of the group. Some people adopt a passive stance, waiting and hoping for someone to notice them or for an opening in the conversation to say something, yet yielding the focus to a more verbal person. Other people attract attention to themselves by the way they dress or walk. Unusual clothes, bright colors, a radical haircut, a swing of the hips while walking, dramatic hand gestures while talking, an affected accent are all indirect ways of asking for attention. And if any of these behaviors does get the desired attention, the individual will most likely continue it.

Try this experiment. Ask someone you trust to listen to you without interruption for a full five minutes. She or he can look, nod, or smile, but not talk. At the end of five minutes, talk about how it felt to have uninterrupted attention. What were your thoughts and feelings? Now let your friend have five minutes of your undivided attention. Discuss her reaction. What was it like for you to give her this attention? What made it hard or easy?

Providing full attention to others is difficult. Most people are not accustomed to receiving or giving it and are frequently concerned that they will not get their turn if they yield the focus to another person. These problems, however, can be minimized. First, practice giving full attention to others while they talk. Follow these guidelines:

1. Stand or sit fairly close to the person so that you can hear and she or he can see you clearly.
2. Maintain eye contact while the other person talks. You do not have to stare, but keep enough contact so that your eyes are clearly on her.
3. Do not interrupt to talk about yourself, your ideas, opinions, or experiences. (It is tempting to interrupt and say, "What you're saying reminds me of. . . .")

Next, ask for others' full attention. When you need someone's total concentration on what you're about to say, say so. Ask for whatever amount of time you need and place yourself close to the listener. If she or he begins to take the focus, gently but firmly indicate that you are not finished.

Finally, provide opportunities for others to be heard uninterrupted. Give others the attention they need. For instance, when you are having a discussion with an employee, choose a comfortable place to sit, ask that your secretary hold all calls and interruptions, and practice attentive listening skills. In meetings, make it a groundrule that after a problem is presented for discussion, each person must have a chance to respond once before anyone can speak a second time.

Clarifying the Message

Providing full attention to the speaker may minimize the possibility of miscommunication, but it cannot guarantee that the message will be accurately received. To improve communication further, leaders need to learn and practice the following skills in clarification:

1. Eliciting information.
2. Paraphrasing what has been heard.
3. Listening for feelings.

Eliciting information

In the section on full attention, it was suggested that you listen fully, with no interruptions. However, an interruption aimed at gaining more information or clarity is both beneficial and appropriate. Often a person is unclear about an idea or problem; at this point asking a question can help the person sift through confusing information and clarify her or his ideas.

CLOSED AND OPEN QUESTIONS

The quality and quantity of information you receive from a question depend on the kind of question you pose. There are two basic types of questions: closed and open.

Closed questions are those that can be answered with a simple yes or no. They are appropriate when the information you need can be stated briefly. For example:

"Do you like the new office arrangement?"
"Do you have a minute to speak with me?"
"Did you vote for Jimmy Carter in the last election?"
"Is the report typed?"

Open questions are those that require a more lengthy response. They are appropriate when additional, detailed information is needed. For example:

"What do you like best about the new office arrangement?"
"What were your reasons for voting for Jimmy Carter?"
"What steps remain to be done before the report is finished?"

The appropriateness of open and closed questions depends on the situation, the kind of information desired, and your purpose. Often, a combination of both is effective. For example, a closed question can be asked before an open one—"Do you like the new office arrangement?" followed by "What do you like best about it?" Appropriate use of such questions increases the likelihood that messages will be clear.

"WHY" QUESTIONS

"Why" questions are a type of open question intended to explore the rationale behind a statement. Such questions must be used carefully, since they frequently imply a demand for an explanation or a defense of the action. A "why" question may be perceived as judgmental or evaluative and thus can put the respondent on the defensive. Emphasizing certain words in the question can augment or alleviate the evaluative effect. Read this sentence with emphasis on the italicized words:

> "*Why* did you organize your report that way?"
> "Why did *you* organize your report that way?"
> "Why did you *organize* your report that way?"
> "Why did you organize your report *that* way?"

Although the demand for an explanation is implied in each sentence, the nature of the explanation required changes as the stressed word changes. A harsh tone of voice for the first sentence could be perceived as being more critical than it would be if asked calmly. The emphasis on the word "you" could be perceived as a personal attack. The third and fourth sentences emphasize a critique of chosen methodology. The shift in emphasis carries an implied meaning.

Remember that people may become defensive if they perceive they are to be evaluated. In such a situation, morale is threatened. Also, defensive followers tend to perform less efficiently than do nondefensive followers. To avoid such consequences, effective leaders change their approach, obtaining the same information without using a "why" question. For example: "I'd be interested in hearing your reasons for organizing the report the way you did."

Observe how frequently others ask "why" questions and note people's reactions to them. Are they defensive—verbally or nonverbally? Check yourself for how frequently you ask "why" questions. Ask yourself if there might be a better way to present your question. Your goal, remember, is to gather more information and to clarify ideas.

Paraphrasing

Paraphrasing is the receiver's repetition, in her own words, of the content of the message in order to check out the success of the communication cycle. To understand this process, select a small group to discuss a problem or topic and follow these rules:

1. Each time you wish to speak, you must first repeat in your own words the previous speaker's statement. This repetition, in your own words, is paraphrasing.
2. Once you have paraphrased the previous speaker's statement, secure her confirmation that your paraphrase was an accurate restatement of what she said.
3. If the speaker says that your paraphrase was not accurate, try again until you get her okay or ask her to restate the point. Paraphrase again until you have done so to her satisfaction.

4. Make your contribution only when your paraphrasing has been accepted by the speaker.
5. The next person who wishes to speak must accurately paraphrase you and *receive your okay* before speaking.

This process will at first feel unnatural. As you become more skilled and learn when paraphrasing is appropriate, you will find it to be an important communication skill. If, for example, you are not sure you heard the speaker correctly, you can stop the process and say, "I'm not really clear on what you said. Did you say . . . ?" The speaker can then agree with your restatement or correct any misunderstandings.

Paraphrasing is especially useful during arguments or discussions of highly emotional issues when one side tends to prepare a rebuttal while the other side is still speaking. Usually, the opposing point of view is only partially heard. Paraphrasing ensures that both sides really listen because each must be able to restate the other's position. Obviously, both sides must agree to adhere to the "rules." The resulting communication is usually clearer and more effective and the relationship between participants is frequently enhanced.

As with any skill, paraphrasing must be used selectively; its overuse or inappropriate use can backfire. To prevent this, always assess your reason for using paraphrase and be sure it fits the situation. Let others know why you are using it so you do not create confusion or resentment.

Listening for feelings

Another communication skill important for leaders is listening for feelings. To understand the relationship between thoughts and feelings, listen to someone else talk. Note what you think you heard the person say and also what you think she or he was feeling at that time. The point is that thoughts and feelings operate simultaneously; while it is often difficult to separate them, doing so can improve communication.

Try the following exercise. Pretend that you are listening to a colleague who says:

"I have been working on this report all morning and still am not finished. It is due at three o'clock today in Mr. Sterling's office. He needs it in time to review it and take it to the cabinet meeting tomorrow. My problem is that I have too much data and haven't determined the best way to organize it. I have outlined three different approaches but can't make up my mind which to use."

Do not reread the paragraph above. Paraphrase what you "heard" and repeat it to your colleague. Start with "I heard you say that. . . ."

Now reread the statement to see if you added your own interpretations to the paraphrase.

Next, try to imagine how the colleague is feeling and express your interpretation. You might say, "I imagine that you are feeling:

". . . frustrated that you have only a limited amount of time to complete the project."
". . . angry that you didn't leave more time to get it written."
". . . confused about which approach would have the best impact on your boss."
". . . overwhelmed because you have other work that needs your attention."

Always check with the speaker to see if you have accurately interpreted both the content and feeling aspects of the message.

The skill of listening for feelings is valuable in helping others to clarify the emotions behind their messages. If the feelings are strong and negative, as in the example, effective communication is inhibited. When you encourage others to identify and express their feelings, you help them reduce the potency of their emotions and thus function more rationally.

Women have been socialized to attend to the needs of others and to seek others' approval of their thoughts and behaviors. As a result, they often let other people's opinions influence how they feel and have difficulty separating the content of messages from others' approval of them. In the example given above, the person facing the decision about how to complete the report could have complicated the situation by letting her feelings about the problem dominate her thinking. She needs to recognize what she is feeling and then separate those feelings from her thinking so that she can proceed.

Situations like this put women into a double bind. On the one hand, women interested in leadership have been encouraged to retain the "feminine" qualities that make up their identity. However, the realities of the working world restrict the utilization of some of these characteristics, suggesting that women need to "become like men" in order to succeed. Take, for example, crying. While it is a normal, healthy expression of emotion, it is rarely understood or accepted by men in a work setting. Marcille Gray Williams in *The New Executive Woman*[1] notes that the women executives she interviewed cried publicly either once or not at all during their careers! When they did, the results were negative—both for them and for the men who saw them. The women were usually embarrassed by their own behavior, and were given the message by those around them, men and women, that crying was inappropriate. The men were clearly uncomfortable with the tears. She points out that most men are better trained to deal with anger than with crying and therefore feel uncomfortable at such an expression of emotions. She suggests that women learn to channel their emotions into anger in order to avoid rejection by male colleagues.

There is no easy answer to this dilemma. The hope is that women leaders can retain their gift for listening for feelings, both in others and in themselves, and use it appropriately as the situation demands.

Speaking Out

Because verbal communication is basic to working with others, women in leadership positions need to express themselves clearly, speak persuasively, and command the attention of others. Think about types of verbal communications. Some are formal presentations and speeches. Many are informal, such as verbal directions to those you supervise or sharing of information with colleagues, subordinates, or bosses.

These speaking experiences may not always be comfortable or successful for you. Perhaps you have found yourself sitting in meetings, rehearsing in your head what you wanted to say until either you lost heart or someone else beat you out with an idea. Perhaps you have found yourself trying to express your ideas or opinions only to have them come out jumbled and confused. Perhaps you have presented an organized and clearly expressed report only to have others ignore or dismiss what you said. Effective speaking skills can be developed. To improve both your informal and formal speaking styles, focus on three aspects of speaking: (1) clarity, (2) organization, and (3) practice.

Be clear

Effective speakers are clear about the purpose of their message. Yet many speakers mumble, jumble, and bungle what they say, going off on tangents, leaving out points, or forgetting what they started. Being clear on what needs to be said and why minimizes these ineffective speaking practices.

Lack of clarity is frequently related to fear. Implicit in speaking out is the risk that others may disagree, discount, ignore, ridicule, or otherwise react negatively. If the speaker lets the fear dominate, she can become momentarily paralyzed, hesitant, withdrawn, or defensive. One way to overcome this fear is to ask yourself, "What is the worst thing that could happen if I spoke out?" You will usually discover that even the worst consequence is a remote possibility. Such a reality check defuses the fear and allows you to participate.

Fear also diminishes as your trust in your own ideas and intelligence increases. Believing that your thoughts and values are sound and worthy of notice is the foundation for effective speaking. Several suggestions to improve your self-concept are found in the last chapter of this book.

As noted earlier, women have been socialized to seek others' approval; the fear that this approval will be withheld, or conditional, can affect how they speak. For instance, the woman who hesitates to introduce an innovative idea in a meeting because she assumes others will think it is ridiculous discounts her creativity and intelligence and denies the group a potentially useful idea. The key word here is "assumes." How do you assume people will react? If you are frequently concerned with others' reactions, you need to develop more confidence in your own judgment and approval. If you find yourself hesitating to speak, check your feelings and then repeat several times to yourself: "I know what *I* want to say and I *can* say it." This statement may sound contrived, but the act of repeating it will help you ferret out uncertainties and fears so that you can deliver a clear message. Knowing what you want to say—and believing in your ability to be clear—improves your communication style.

Again, when you want to counter your fears and dependency on others' approval, repeat to yourself: "I know what *I* want to say and I *can* say it." Take a deep breath, sit or stand proudly, and speak out. The more you trust your own abilities, the more confidence you will instill in others. With time, you won't need to prepare yourself for action; instead, you will more quickly recognize what you want to say and be able to speak out clearly.

Organize your thoughts

To achieve an effective speaking style, you must organize your thoughts. Even if you are clear about what you want to say, recovering the required information from your human "computer" may take a little time. When you find yourself initially stumped, stall for time so you can organize your thoughts. For instance, when Joanne's boss unexpectedly asked for her reaction to the meeting they had just left, she needed a few minutes to organize her thoughts coherently. She responded, "Can you be more specific?" While her boss rephrased the question, Joanne not only learned more about the intended focus of the question but also gained time to prepare a clear response. This is an example of spontaneous organizing.

Listen to people you consider to be good speakers as they talk formally or informally at presentations or meetings. You can probably recognize an often used organizational style in which the speaker told you what she or he was going to say, proceeded to say it, and then summarized the key points. This pattern is usually more obvious in a prepared talk, but even those speaking informally convey a sense of organization by following a logical sequence.

While men are considered to be skilled in logical thinking, women are not. Yet women have both the experience in organizing and the intelligence needed to ensure a coherent and logical speaking style. You may have had limited formal speaking opportunities that demanded a carefully prepared outline; still, you probably have organized your thoughts for papers in school and for projects at work and in your personal life. These experiences provide a foundation for organizing your verbal messages in a logical manner.

One of the best tools to use when you give a formal report or speech is the outline. As you probably once learned in school, a presentation needs an opening, a body, and a conclusion. Each part has its own purpose and is crucial to an organized presentation.

The opening functions as an attention getter and introduces listeners to your topic. Attention and interest can be captured by a pertinent quotation or story, a question or challenging statement, a generalization appropriate to your topic, or an object or picture. The body of your presentation contains the main ideas, which also must be organized. If you plan to cover three major points, present each one to your listeners briefly. This preview gives them an organizational scheme to follow your line of thinking. In other words, delineate the scope of your presentation and then expand on each point with details and evidence. In your conclusion briefly review the ideas presented. If appropriate, you can also suggest how the audience can use the information provided.

Practice

Effective public speakers like Barbara Jordan, the Texas politician, and Flo Kennedy, the New York attorney and civil rights activist, were not born that way; they learned and practiced and practiced some more. If you hope to enhance either your informal or formal speaking ability, you must practice. Improvement can be made in several ways:

1. Prepare your verbal presentations in outline form and practice with someone you trust or with a tape recorder and a mirror.

2. Ask people for feedback on your public speaking. Tell them your particular concern—such as articulation, organization, or effectiveness of openings and conclusions. Good public speaking involves so

many variables that the task may seem overwhelming. Work on your improvement gradually by asking for feedback on only one or two variables at a time. Work on those and then ask for further feedback on additional areas.

3. Join a public speaking club, such as Toastmasters International.[2] Regular meetings provide you with considerable practice in preparing and giving speeches.

4. Hire a speech coach to work with you individually.

Speak out. Don't wait. Confront your fears. Prepare your thoughts. Practice, and reap the benefits of being an effective speaker.

Giving and Receiving Feedback

As a leader, you are in a position to both give and receive feedback—those verbal and nonverbal messages that reaffirm or criticize behaviors, attitudes, and performance. Because your followers look to you for guidance and direction, you must understand the process of giving both positive and negative feedback and its effect on others. Also, because you receive feedback from supervisors, colleagues, and followers, you must understand your feelings and reactions as a recipient.

The style you use in giving and receiving feedback depends on many variables: the way your parents and teachers reacted to you, the ratio of negative to positive reactions you've received in the past, your self-concept and self-confidence, and your attitude toward others. Understanding your style and assessing your success will help you isolate areas that need improvement.

First, assess yourself as a feedback dispenser and receiver on the items presented opposite. Each pair of statements represents two extreme positions. Your attitudes and behavior should fit somewhere between these polarities. As you assess yourself, think about the origins of your feelings and actions as a dispenser and receiver and how they affect your ability as a leader.

Read each item and decide which is most like you. Place a P at a point on the line to indicate the way you give or receive *positive* feedback and an N to indicate the way you give or receive *negative* feedback.

Now, examine your responses and answer the following questions:

1. Do you find it easier to give positive or negative feedback? Why?
2. Do you find it easier to receive positive or negative feedback? Why?
3. What areas do you need to work on to increase your effectiveness as a leader? Try to be as specific as possible in your answer. For example, you may feel you need to be more specific when

Giving Feedback

/ _____/ _____/ _____/ _____/
| I give feedback when | I never give feedback |
| it is not requested. | unless it is requested. |

/ _____/ _____/ _____/ _____/
| I give feedback only | I give feedback any |
| in private. | time, anyplace. |

/ _____/ _____/ _____/ _____/
| I consciously plan times | I spontaneously give |
| to give feedback. | feedback. |

/ _____/ _____/ _____/ _____/
I always give feedback	My feedback usually
directly to the person.	gets to the person
	indirectly.

/ _____/ _____/ _____/ _____/
| My feedback provides | My feedback provides |
| specific information. | general information. |

/ _____/ _____/ _____/ _____/
My negative feedback	I give negative feed-
provides information on	back whether or not the
which the person can actually	other person can do
act and/or change.	anything about it.

/ _____/ _____/ _____/ _____/
| I hate to give feedback. | I love to give feedback. |

Receiving Feedback

/ _____/ _____/ _____/ _____/
| When receiving feedback, | When receiving feedback, |
| I reject or discount it. | accept it. |

/ _____/ _____/ _____/ _____/
When receiving unclear	When receiving unclear
feedback, I ask for more	feedback, I never ask for
information.	more information.

/ _____/ _____/ _____/ _____/
When receiving very	When receiving very general
general feedback, I always	feedback, I never ask for
ask for specifics.	specifics.

/ _____/ _____/ _____/ _____/
When receiving positive	When receiving positive
feedback, I always wonder	feedback, I never question
what "string is attached."	the motive of the giver.

/ _____/ _____/ _____/ _____/
When receiving feedback,	When receiving feedback,
I always reciprocate	I never reciprocate
immediately.	immediately.

/ _____/ _____/ _____/ _____/
| I write down the feedback | I never record the feed- |
| I receive. | back I receive. |

/ _____/ _____/ _____/ _____/
I always ask others for validation of	I never ask others for
the information	validation of the information
I've just received.	I've just received.

/ _____/ _____/ _____/ _____/
I accept and incorporate the	I never accept or incor-
feedback I receive into my	porate the feedback I
behavior.	receive into my behavior.

/ _____/ _____/ _____/ _____/
| I hate to receive feedback. | I love to receive feedback. |

you give feedback. Or you may feel you need to check out the negative feedback you receive with others for accuracy.

Feedback and leadership

Because both positive and negative feedback are essential to leadership, women must learn to use them appropriately and effectively. Effective leaders are skilled in giving and receiving negative and positive feedback. They understand that failing to give someone constructive criticism is a disservice to that person, to other subordinates, and to the organization. At the same time, they recognize that providing negative feedback without balancing it with positive feedback decreases motivation and willingness to learn and closes communication channels. Finally, effective leaders are able to accept feedback from others without anger or embarrassment.

Feedback plays a powerful role in human behavior. It can motivate, encourage, and redirect others toward new and better work behaviors. It can also help people learn from successes and failures. To be effective, feedback must fit the situation. The leader must assess the work environment and know her people, the cultural norms of the organization, and the basic principles of human behavior before determining how, when, where, and what feedback is appropriate. As the expression "Different strokes for different folks" suggests, people are unique and need individualized feedback. To determine what a person needs, ask yourself these questions:

—How comfortable is the person in receiving this kind of information?
—Is the person used to receiving this kind of information?
—What is the best time and place to give this person feedback?

Men, women, and feedback

Men and women have been socialized differently, so they have different leadership styles that influence their effectiveness as givers and receivers of both negative and positive feedback. Men tend to be more comfortable with giving negative feedback. They have learned to control their emotions rigidly and often have difficulty giving positive information to others. Some men feel that employees should be given positive feedback only for superior work, that routine work does not deserve positive affirmation. Yet, some men readily give negative feedback when employees do not meet their expectations or standards.

Women, on the other hand, tend to be more comfortable with giving positive feedback. Because of their socialization, they find it important to please others and to gain their approval. As a result, they often overplay the positive and underplay the negative. Women find it easy to give others many kinds of positive reassurances and accolades. Yet they may go to great lengths to avoid giving negative feedback or to cushion it through generalities and indirectness.

On the receiving end, women tend to be more comfortable than men in hearing positive feedback. Historically, however, much of the positive information women have received relates to their bodies, not to their accomplishments. Women have learned to accept positive information about their physical selves more readily than about their intelligence or creativity.

Women tend to be less comfortable than men in receiving negative feedback, perhaps because of their need for others' approval. Some women take negative feedback too personally. That is, they see the feedback as an indication that they themselves, rather than their ideas or performance, need improvement. This, in turn, makes them reluctant to give negative feedback to others. The woman leader may, therefore, unconsciously protect others from negative feedback because she herself does not like to hear such information. Women in leadership positions must learn to separate the content of the feedback from their emotional reactions.

To test out these ideas about men, women, and feedback, try this experiment. For the next few days, observe how men and women act when giving and receiving both positive and negative feedback. Intentionally give positive feedback to men and women, on both their appearance and their achievements. Note what happens when men and women give negative feedback to others and what happens when it is given to them. As you observe, take notes and look for similarities and differences. Anticipate how you might have reacted in similar circumstances. Hold your judgments about the appropriateness of each person's actions until you've finished reading this section.

Positive feedback

Most people are hungry for affirmation of their worth and accomplishments. Why are people so desperate for positive feedback? Probably because they never received enough as they were growing up. Well-meaning parents, teachers, and other adults in their lives did not recognize this need or were unable or unwilling to fulfill it.

Think about a toddler who follows her parent around, latching onto the parent's legs, making noises, and crying. The toddler wants attention and reassurance and is quite direct in her efforts to receive positive feedback. As she grows up, she learns that it is not appropriate to demand so much attention from her parents and others around her.

She begins to suppress the demand and even the desire for positive affirmation, but the need does not disappear. Instead, she is socialized to seek this positive affirmation indirectly or to accept whatever she gets.

It is important for leaders to recognize that the people they work with need and want positive affirmation. Positive feedback increases subordinates' self-esteem, builds on their strengths, and enhances positive and open feelings toward others. As a leader, encourage others to accept the positive feedback they receive and to guard against discounting it—that is, belittling or denying the accuracy of the feedback. For example, the person who responds to positive feedback on a report by saying, "But I did that in only an hour," is discounting the feedback. As a leader, model a style that both gives and receives positive affirmation.

Below are several groundrules to ensure the acceptance of positive feedback. As you read them, apply them first to yourself and then to others.

Do not deny the feedback. The receiver of positive feedback must not deny its accuracy. The giver of the compliment has perceived the receiver in a positive way, and any denial implies that her or his perception is inaccurate. If you give a positive stroke and the receiver discounts or denies it, ask the person to listen and repeat it.

Accept it totally. A simple way to accept is to say, "Thank you." A more humorous way is to say, "How perceptive of you to notice." This is likely to make the receiver laugh.

Plan on it. Consciously decide to make a specific number of positive statements to others every day. Look for opportunities to make them. Also, plan on receiving a certain number each day. You may have to ask for them, and that's okay. In both cases, increase your quota as the original number becomes a habit and is done with ease.

Write them down. As you notice something you like about an employee's work or behavior, make a note of it. Tell the employee and file the note in her folder. Write positive comments directly on others' memos or reports. The extra minute you take can do wonders for them and for you. When you receive compliments, write them down and store them in a "rainy day" folder that you can refer to when you feel low or doubtful of your abilities. Or write them on an index card and carry it with you in your purse to serve as your "insurance card against depression."

Give and get reinforcement. Reinforce your comments by repeating them at later points. Positive feedback is more likely to be accepted if it is given more than once. As a receiver, ask for reinforcing feedback, particularly in areas where you need reassurance.

How can you ensure that those you work with receive sufficient positive feedback?

To begin with, discuss the need for positive affirmation in your work group and determine ways to provide it. Agree among yourselves to meet that need. At the beginning of your meetings with subordinates, have each employee share one success that she or he had since the last meeting. If the group is unfamiliar with routine public affirmation, have people speak in order around the table rather than randomly. Asking for volunteers may result in silence! At the end of a meeting or conference, have each person share something she or he appreciates about someone else. These comments can be sentence completions, such as "I appreciated _____ for _____."

When employees turn a report in to you, ask them to tell you what they liked about their work. And be sure to let your boss know about your employees' accomplishments. When your boss visits your area, introduce her or him to some of your employees. At each introduction, point out something positive about both the boss and the subordinate.

Try this exercise at a group meeting. Distribute a copy of the Stroke Collection (#5) to each person present and have the employee put her or his name on it. Pass the papers around the group and have each member circle a word describing the person whose name is on the paper. The first person receiving the paper chooses from the first group of descriptors, the second person from the second group of descriptors, and so on. The owner eventually receives her or his paper back with six circled words.

Negative feedback

How many times have you heard people say, "I have to tell you something for your own good"? Many people assume that negative feedback is for the receiver's own good when it is often for the benefit of the giver! An effective leader must determine if the feedback is important, assess the circumstances and individuals involved, and select the most appropriate means of giving the negative information.

The giver of feedback must explore how the receiver will benefit in order to make the interaction meaningful. Ask yourself: "What type of feedback will be in this person's best interests?" A chronically late employee will not change her behavior if she sees no value in getting to work on time. Instead of just criticizing the employee, you should help her identify the benefits of being on time and of learning from her mistakes, all in the context of professional growth.

People need both negative and positive feedback to determine if their work is productive. For example, when a typist reads a document

5   THE STROKE COLLECTION

Name _____

Date _____

A.		D.	
1.	Supportive	1.	Tender
2.	Kind	2.	Responsible
3.	Attentive	3.	Alive
4.	Cooperative	4.	Steadfast
5.	Stimulating	5.	Forthright
6.	Enthusiastic	6.	Reasonable
7.	Trustworthy	7.	Loving
8.	Perceptive	8.	Insightful
9.	Wise	9.	Energetic
10.	Warm	10.	Uplifting

B.		E.	
1.	Reassuring	1.	Honest
2.	Encouraging	2.	Trusting
3.	Dependable	3.	Friendly
4.	Loyal	4.	Right-on
5.	Thoughtful	5.	Deferential
6.	Considerate	6.	Positive
7.	Influential	7.	Arousing
8.	Affectionate	8.	Useful
9.	Vital	9.	Sympathetic
10.	Tactful	10.	Aware

C.		F.	
1.	Zestful	1.	Neat
2.	Helpful	2.	Cool
3.	Accepting	3.	Delightful
4.	Refreshing	4.	Empathic
5.	Generous	5.	Inspiring
6.	Thorough	6.	Zealous
7.	Valuable	7.	Clever
8.	Sensitive	8.	Reliable
9.	Ardent	9.	Open
10.	Creative	10.	Astute

just typed, she or he gets feedback on the quality of the work. If there are mistakes, they can be corrected. Similarly, a mechanic gets feedback on a reassembled motor when she or he starts it. Without such feedback, mistakes may not be recognized.

People react differently to negative feedback. Some of your followers will become defensive, adopting a passive stance or striking back with negative comments or actions. What causes such a reaction to negative feedback? Recall a time when you felt defensive. Think about what was said to you, how you were feeling, and what you were thinking. What was it about the situation that made you feel defensive? Most likely it included one or several of these elements:

1. You perceived that you were being evaluated.
2. You sensed that the other person had control over you.
3. You felt inferior to the other person.
4. You were not ready to hear the information or wanted to deny that it was true.

If an employee becomes defensive, aggressive, or passive when you give negative feedback, try to understand what she or he is feeling. Pointing out these feelings may help the person talk about them. Do not ignore the employee's reaction. It must be dealt with if the feedback is to produce positive results.

GIVING NEGATIVE FEEDBACK

Here are some groundrules for giving negative feedback:

Have a rationale. Be sure you know why the negative feedback is needed to accomplish a task or improve the morale of the group. Be sure it's not because of your own hang-ups or psychological needs. Understand your motive, then develop a fair rationale.

Determine the best time and place to give the feedback. Be sure you know as much as possible about the situation: the employee's attitude toward the work and toward receiving feedback at the time; how often the person has heard the information before; and if the general climate in the organization and in your work unit is conducive to learning a result of a feedback session.

Do it directly and privately. Never give feedback indirectly through someone else or in writing. The receiver deserves a full explanation from you. Others should be present only if the interaction affects them. Otherwise, preserve the employee's dignity with privacy.

Plan what you intend to say. Isolate the problem and think through how you will say it. Limit the feedback to that which is important now. In other words, don't bring in past errors; stick to the present. If you are anxious about the encounter, practice the interchange with someone you trust or on a tape recorder.

Limit your criticism to reality. Discuss only those actions or behaviors that the receiver can change. Negative feedback on problems beyond a person's control does not benefit anyone.

Do not delay. Speaking up becomes more difficult when you postpone it. If you wait, you may build up excessive anger or resentment or you may suppress your anger and simply ignore the negative behavior.

Describe the problem in specific terms. Generalities do not motivate people to change. Be specific and cite examples. Use descriptive, not evaluative, terms.

Do unto others. Think about how you'd like to receive negative feedback and act accordingly.

In order to give negative feedback in a nonthreatening, meaningful way, you must decrease your own discomfort with negative feedback. Model a positive approach for others. You might also hold a workshop with your employees to deal with the topic. Explore their feelings about negative feedback, determine the best approach to dealing with criticism, and establish groundrules for all to observe.

Work out a system by which employees can ask for feedback. People are more receptive to feedback when they request it. The chances are greater that the feedback will produce positive results if there is a mechanism to encourage it. Schedule informal meetings to discuss critical issues and problems and to allow employees to air their complaints. Assign a rulekeeper at these meetings to make sure no groundrules are violated. Rotate this role so that the responsibility is shared.

RESPONDING TO NEGATIVE FEEDBACK

Leaders must expect to receive feedback from those around them—bosses, followers, and colleagues. Since many of these people are men who have been socialized to communicate with a great deal of criticism and challenge, women need to understand their own style of responding to negative feedback and to assess the appropriateness of their responses.

How do you respond when you are criticized? Do you (1) throw the criticism back to the giver, (2) argue with the critic, (3) collapse in tears or some other expression of emotion, or (4) accept the feedback passively? Each of these responses is explained below. As you read, keep the following questions in mind:

1. How does your response benefit you? Behavioral patterns

persist as long as they serve a person's self-interest. What is yours?

2. Are you satisfied with your pattern of response? What would you like to change or to keep?

Throwback. A person may throw the criticism back to the giver as a form of denial. If you tend to do this, try to break the pattern. Be open to the possibility that you may in fact have been in error. "Yes, you're right. I did make a mistake." These words may be very difficult to say, but they are essential to breaking the throwback pattern. Once you say them, do not fall back into retaliatory criticism.

Argument. The arguer denies the words of the critic, offering a logical rebuttal to every negative remark. Or the arguer may partially agree before denying by saying, "Yes, but. . . ." The emphasis is really on the "but." If you are an arguer, slow down to make sure you fully understand what the other person is saying. The skill of paraphrasing, presented earlier in this chapter, is helpful here because it forces you to listen closely and repeat what is being said before you present your side.

Collapse. A collapser reacts with tears, a cracking voice, or a shaking body. People who collapse tend to take criticism "hook, line, and sinker." You needn't be devastated by criticism, because what is said may not be totally true. Evaluate others' judgments against your own self-knowledge. When you receive negative criticism, ask yourself, "How true is this about me?" Keep in mind that you are the ultimate judge of what is true and not true about you.

Passive acceptance. The passive accepter, like the collapser, accepts what is said to her as the "truth" with words of acquiescence like, "Yes, you're right." If you do this, challenge the accuracy of the criticism and reclaim your right to judge what is best for you.

What can you do to improve your ability to handle negative feedback? Start by determining the areas where *you* want and need to hear feedback. Be clear on these areas so that when you are reviewed on your performance you can indicate specifically where you'd like help. This shows a positive attitude toward your own growth. Ask for feedback frequently from people you trust. Have them tell you about areas in which you need to grow.

Let people know if the timing of the feedback is wrong for you. If you are especially tired or low in spirits, or if the giver is emotionally high, ask for a delay until you both are in a better mood for hearing each other. Make sure that you get back to the critic within 48 hours.

Listen while you are being criticized and look at the critic. Ask for more information and for specific examples if necessary. Keep asking questions, because the first statements of criticism are often not the most important; they are openers for the underlying issue.

Keep a record of the negative criticism you receive. You may find a pattern which makes it clear that you do have a problem, even if you have been denying it. Develop a plan to work on the problem. Set a deadline and record your progress. If possible, share your progress with your original critics. Remember that mistakes are a part of living and that you can learn from all of them. Reward yourself each time you handle negative feedback more rationally.

As a leader, you need to continually develop your communication skills. The communication cycle goes on and on. It is up to you to develop the skills you need for your current leadership position and to carry them with you in whatever future positions you hold.

Communication in the Organization

Leaders must improve their ability to communicate not only within their own work unit but also within the entire organization. Your own work unit does not function independently of the rest of the organization. Successful leaders learn about and utilize both the formal and informal communication channels.

Woman are less familiar than men with the broad perspectives of an organization, though they are generally quite adept at taking care of the "home front." As women ascend the organizational ladder, they must become more knowledgeable about the entire picture. The process is similar to the stages of growing up. Infants and young children are initially concerned only about themselves and, later, about their own family. As they begin to interact with other children, the world expands for them. The circle grows even wider as they become aware of their immediate community, then their nation, and finally the world. As adults, they are concerned about their own family circle as well as events that occur worldwide. The mature adult knows how much world events can affect her or his personal life. In a similar way, a developing leader must understand how the organization as a whole operates.

The organizational pyramid

Most organizations are structured in a hierarchical pyramid. The majority of employees are at the bottom, a minority are in the middle, and a select few are at the top. Communication flows up and down definite lines within the pyramid. These lines can vary from organization to organization, as Figure 3 shows. The number of people at different levels of responsibility changes, but the structure, with its definite top and bottom, remains the same.

Figure 3. Organizational structures.

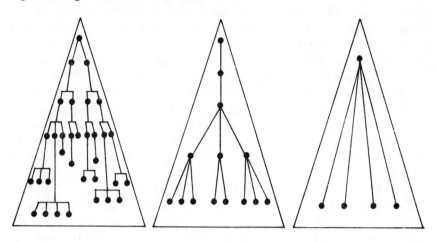

To analyze your own organization, obtain or draw a table that identifies formal roles in their hierarchical order and connects them to the formal lines of communication—that is, the ways used to relay policies, directives, and reports. Think of them as radio channels. A message goes along a specific channel with no deviation; it must pass point A before going to point B. Formal lines of communication are established to ensure orderliness and authority and tend to be quite rigid. Think about recent information you received in your organization. What parts were disseminated along formal lines? Was the information written or verbal, one to one or in groups?

At the beginning of this chapter we examined the interpersonal and organizational communication skills needed by leaders at all levels of the organization. As you review those skills, remember that the responsibility for setting policy and determining the overall structures of the organization rests with the top managers, who also establish the communication climate for the organization. Middle managers are responsible for establishing networks or procedures to carry out the policy set by the top managers. As intermediaries in the organization, they serve as conduits of information to and from levels above and below them. They rely heavily on informal communication. Leaders at the lower levels are responsible for informing their subordinates of policies and communications they receive from higher levels.

Even if you are at the lower levels of your organization, you need to know how communication flows in the whole organization. There are several reasons for this. First, you need to be aware of how the whole system operates in order to understand your position relative to other positions. Second, if you know the communication networks, you can utilize them for your own needs. Third, you may not always be at the bottom of the hierarchy. If you plan to move up to the middle and top levels of management, you must understand the roles that higher-level leaders play in the total communication structure.

An effective leader learns how communication flows in the organization and systematically taps these flows. To do this, the leader must explore the informal methods of communication that develop in all organizations; it is often through these networks that crucial information is conveyed. The "old boy network," for example, is an informal system that has considerable power: If you're "in," you get the needed information; if you're "out," you are left in the dark. Ideas on how to get "in" are examined below.

The following exercise, based on a model used by Michael Korda,[3] can help you understand how informal networks of communication work. Place a piece of tracing paper over the diagram you've obtained (or drawn) of your organization's formal structure. Think about the influence that different people in the organization possess. Draw circles of varying sizes to symbolize people's personal power. Obviously, the person with the most power will have the largest circle. As you continue, notice that you are adding circles that usually do not appear on the diagram. The additional circles may be for secretaries and custodians. Such people often have considerable power and influence and are an integral part of the informal communication network. Next, draw lines to connect the circles. Vary the width of the lines to symbolize the strength of the communication between individuals. When you finish the diagram, you will see that the lines of informal communication do not necessarily flow along the formal lines. The flow includes different people and channels.

Informal networks

Informal networks of communication are active and changing in all organizations and supply a variety of information to their members, such as the latest gossip about interpersonal conflicts or affairs, inside information on job openings or terminations, information on relevant articles in professional journals, notices of conferences or workshops, and previews of organizational problems. Access to this information is crucial if a leader is to stay informed of the comings and goings of the organization and to take advantage of opportunities for professional growth.

How can you top this informal communication system? Take note of where influential people spend their informal time—that is, when they are not at their desks or in conference. When the boss takes a coffeebreak, where does she or he go? Does the boss roam around, stopping regularly at certain people's offices or work areas? Who spends time with the powerful people? Who rides to work together? Who goes to lunch together?

The first step, then, is to become an astute observer of powerful people, those who are most likely to have, hold, and pass along useful information. Observe their routine behavior for a few weeks. Next, gradually move into areas frequented by these people. For instance:

—Take your coffeebreak at the same time they do.

—Drop into their offices on any pretext.

—As they walk by your office, call them in for a moment of conversation.

—Invite yourself to lunch with the group. Say, "Where are you all having lunch? I'd like to go along today."

—Get rides to and from work periodically, if not regularly, with them.

—Join in the social events. Go to birthday parties, TGIFs, social hours, baseball games, bowling and golf leagues, and holiday parties.

Another way to ease yourself into informal networks is to tap the gossip system. As you mingle among the employees of your organization (and don't exclude the secretaries and custodians, who know more than managers ever imagine), listen to what they say. Repeat, *listen*. Don't embellish, substantiate, or challenge what is said. In other words, don't contribute to the gossip; just absorb and sift through the information for fact versus fiction. If possible, check the source of the gossip. Since you know the influential people and their relationships to others, you can probably trace the gossip back to the originator.

Suppose your boss's secretary casually mentions that Mr. Samuels, head of marketing, is looking for a new job. Is this fact or rumor? It's important to know the source of this information. You recall that the secretary giving you the tip and Mr. Samuels' secretary carpool to work together; thus it is likely that they have discussed this in the car. You can also assume that Mr. Samuels' secretary knows the content of phone calls and conferences that occur inside the boss's office. So through the two secretaries you may gain access to unofficial information. If this information is accurate, and you have your eye on Mr. Samuels' job, then you can prepare yourself for an upward move. If, however, you know that the secretary who is the source of the information loves to gossip or dislikes her boss and wishes he would leave, you better check the information out further.

Remember that the informal pipeline in the hierarchy works both ways, so that those at the lower levels pass up information as well. You can be sure that your actions, conflicts, and mistakes, as well as achievements, are being observed. If you are competent, that fact will most likely be passed along the informal channels. You may even receive feedback from someone several levels above you who says, "I've been hearing good things about you." If you know how the pipeline works, you can feed information about your aspirations and accomplishments into it so the right people will hear about you.

A third way to tape the informal communication system is through the written word. Read notices on all bulletin boards regularly. They contain a wealth of information, including job notices, announcements of educational opportunities and conferences, items for sale, and requests for information. You can also post notices on the bulletin board to get information you need and to keep visible. Bulletin boards often contain information that is available nowhere else. One saleswoman, for example, was trying to meet a potential client who had just been hired, but did not know her name. A habitual bulletin board reader, she happened upon a newspaper account of this woman that gave her not only the prospect's name but enough other information to make their first conference fruitful.

Get on the routing slips of important trade and professional journals. Notice which ones appear in the offices of influential people. Borrow their copies to determine what is useful to you. Ask them to add you to the list, emphasizing how anxious you are to keep informed. This expressed interest may spur them to put you higher up on the list so that you receive the current issue this month instead of next month. Ask these influential people to watch for certain articles for you in particular publications. This way, you may get a publication even before your name comes up on the routing slip.

One supervisor of five people has a system for determining the order in which she routes magazines, articles, reports, and conference notices. Those highest on her list are the people who have expressed an interest in increasing their professional knowledge and a willingness to read what she sends promptly. Their behavior has "trained" her to send them the information first. In a similar fashion, you can "train" others to keep you in mind when useful information comes across their desks.

Get copies of reports that are not normally or routinely distributed. When you hear that a certain report has been completed and think you would benefit from reading it, try to obtain a copy. If copies are not kept in an area accessible to all employees, ask someone diplomatically if you can borrow a copy. Don't be afraid to ask. The worst that can happen is that you will be told "no."

Create your own communication system

As a leader, you usually have the authority to develop some of your own mechanisms for communication within your work unit. What types of communication should you use?

duce employee morale and initiative. Employees like to be asked their opinions when they know the topic or problem and when they are personally affected. The two-way method involves employees directly and thus enhances morale and encourages initiation. However, this method is slower than one-way communication and leaves the sender vulnerable to challenge.

Which system should you use? Both. Determine your purpose and be selective. Ask yourself each time:

—Are speed and efficiency important?
—What will be the effect on employees?
—How difficult is the material?
—Am I overusing a particular method?

VERBAL OR WRITTEN?

Communication can be verbal or written. As a leader, consider the advantages and disadvantages of both. Like one- and two-way communication, the appropriateness of verbal or written forms depends on the situation. Before you decide on a method to convey a particular message, review the questions listed above on one- and two-way communication.

Assess your abilities as a verbal and written communicator. In which are you stronger? In what ways are you stronger? How can you improve your skill in the other form? Check your clarity and accuracy in verbal and written communication with colleagues and employees. Emphasize your strengths and work on your weaknesses. Leaders should be skilled in both types of communication so they can function well in a variety of situations.

INDIVIDUAL OR GROUP?

Messages can be conveyed to an individual or to a group. Once again, as a leader, you need to decide which method best serves your purpose. Here are some guidelines:

—Use one-to-one communication to discipline, to provide negative feedback, or to counsel an employee.
—Use group communication when information must be given to everyone. Cover only the points that are essential to all. Having employees listen to reports and discussions unrelated to their work is a waste of time, energy, and money.
—Use one-to-one communication to issue instructions or hold discussions that are pertinent to only one employee.
—Use both one-to-one and group communication to praise people's work and behavior. (More extensive information on group

ONE-WAY OR TWO-WAY?

Communication can be sent through one-way or tw
both of which a leader should use. Recall a one-way
sent to you, such as a memo instructing you to do s
certain date or to obtain information and send it back to
Similar one-way messages are given in PA announceme
meetings when the boss announces a policy and allows n

Now recall a two-way communication in which the se
to face with you and was interested in your questions or
clarification. Recall a written two-way communication suc
asking you to respond through a phone call, a follow-up
conference.

Compare the two types of communication systems by
the following:

	One-way Communication	Two-? Communi
1. Which is faster?	_____	_____
2. Which appears to be more efficient?	_____	_____
3. Which enhances morale?	_____	_____
4. Which allows for initiation?	_____	_____
5. Which is better for material that is:		
New, difficult, ambiguous?	_____	_____
Familiar, previously understood?	_____	_____
6. Which ensures greater accuracy?	_____	_____

As you can see, both types of communication are useful in cer
situations. When you need a fast, efficient method to convey infor
tion that is fairly familiar to the recipients, the one-way method
usually appropriate. The two-way method of communication is app
priate when you want to be sure that information has been understo
thoroughly.

Each system has its advantages and disadvantages. The one-wa
method protects the sender's power, authority, and leadership statu
Because no dialogue is possible, the sender is insulated from direc
challenge or blame. However, frequent use of the one-way system can

communication and running effective meetings is provided in Chapter 4.)

COMMUNICATION NETWORKS

Communication networks vary in kind, size, and purpose, as Figure 4 shows. Networks I and II operate without a designated leader. In I, communication flows from person to person, with eventual completion of the circle. In II, information is passed down the line, requiring those in the middle (B, C, and D) to serve as conduits. When the information reaches the end (A and E), communication flows in the other direction.

Networks of this type have certain disadvantages. In II, for example, the people at the ends sometimes never get the message; they are purposely or inadvertently left out. In both I and II, the absence of an identifiable leader can lead to inefficient and incomplete communication. When a task must be accomplished, a leader is needed to provide direction. In addition, only minimal interaction among group members takes place.

In the direct communication network (III), each employee communicates directly to the leader (L). This method works well when the number of employees is not large or when the leader needs to monitor the work of others closely. The indirect methods (IV and V) require the employee to report to an intermediary, who then reports to the leader. When the number of employees is large, this form of communication and supervision increases efficiency because it enables the leader to pursue other executive tasks and to delegate day-to-day operations to the intermediaries. This method, however, decreases the leader's direct contact with employees and allows greater opportunity for miscommunication.

In networks VI, VII, VIII, which can operate within the direct and indirect networks, communication flows both formally and informally among the members of the work group as well as toward the designated leader. The underlying assumption behind such an arrangement is that group members can communicate directly what they know and what their problems are. Group members function as resources for one another. In order for the system to work, therefore, everyone must be interested in and committed to joint problem solving.

This knowledge of how different organizational networks work, informally and formally, can help you expand your own operating arena and build upon basic communication concepts to enhance your leadership skills.

Figure 4. Communication networks.

Leaderless networks

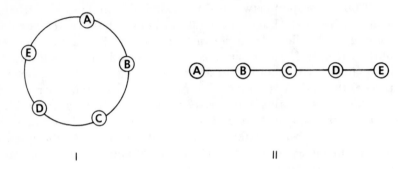

I   II

Direct versus indirect networks

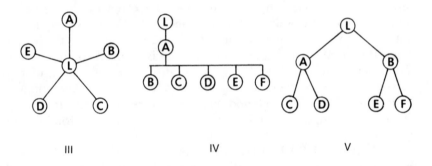

III   IV   V

Interrelated networks

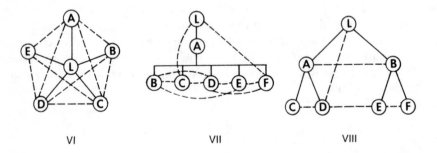

VI   VII   VIII

REFERENCES

1. Marcille Gray Williams, *The New Executive Woman* (Radnor, PA: Chilton Book Company, 1977), pp. 69-82.
2. Toastmasters International, Inc., 2200 N. Grand Avenue, Santa Ana, CA 92711. Write to find out about booklets available from the club nearest you.
3. Michael Korda, *Power! How to Get It, How to Use It* (New York: Ballantine Books, 1975), pp. 107-115.

RESOURCES

General

Buening, Charles. *Communicating on the Job: A Practical Guide for Supervisors.* Reading, MA: Addison-Wesley, 1974.

Jackins, Harvey. *The Human Side of Human Beings: The Theory of Reevaluation Counseling.* Seattle: Rationale Island Publishers, 1972.

Johnson, David W. *Reaching Out: Interpersonal Effectiveness and Self-Actualization* (1976). Available from National Humanistic Education Center, 110 Spring Street, Saratoga Springs, NY 12866.

Majors, Jack. *Communicating the Joy, Pain, and Everything: Insights and Exercises for Communicating in Relationships.* La Jolla, CA: University Associates, 1976.

Simon, Sidney. *Negative Criticism.* Niles, IL: Argus Communications, 1978.

Body Language

Fast, Julius. *Body Language.* New York: Pocket Books, 1971.

Fast, Julius. *The Body Language of Sex, Power, and Aggression.* New York: Harcourt Brace Jovanovich, 1978.

Nierenberg, Gerald I., and Henry H. Calero. *How to Read a Person Like a Book.* New York: Pocket Books, 1973.

Communication in Organizations

Bowers, David G. *Systems of Organizations.* Ann Arbor: University of Michigan Press, 1976.

Harragan, Betty. *Games Mother Never Taught You.* New York: Rawson Associates, 1977.

Korda, Michael. *Power! How to Get It, How to Use It.* New York: Ballantine Books, 1975.

Mintzberg, Henry. "Power In and Around Your Organization." *Training,* October 1977, pp. 35-37.

Speaking

Stone, Janet, and Jane Bachner. *Speaking Up: A Book for Every Woman Who Wants to Speak Effectively.* New York: McGraw-Hill, 1977.

Women and Communications

International Association of Business Communicators. *Without Bias: A Guidebook for Nondiscriminatory Communication.* Available from the association, 870 Market Street, Suite 928, San Francisco, CA 94102.

Pierce, Carol, and Janice Sanfacon. "Man/Woman Dynamics: Some Typical Communication Patterns." In Sargent, Alice G., *Beyond Sex Roles.* San Francisco, CA: West Publishing Co., 1977.

Westbrook, Barbara. *Sex Differences in Human Communication.* New York: Houghton-Mifflin, 1977.

Williams, Marcille Gray. *The New Executive Woman.* Radnor, PA: Chilton Book Company, 1977.

4

Working effectively
with others

WORKING EFFECTIVELY WITH OTHERS is a fundamental skill for leaders. Effective leadership depends on successful and punctual accomplishment of a given task, maintenance of good relationships among followers, and development of positive feelings about the work and members of the work group. This chapter provides you with information on human relations skills that will enhance your effectiveness as a leader.

As previously discussed, leadership skills are highly interdependent. Application of one skill frequently depends on mastery of the others. Thus the skills presented here interact with those in communication for achieving meaningful human relationships, and with those in supervising, making decisions, and planning for accomplishing a task.

What Is Involved in Human Relations?

The individual is the focal point of human relations. Each individual is unique in her or his beliefs, values, and attitudes. It is the leader's responsibility to learn as much as possible about her followers' particular patterns of behavior, as well as her own. Only then can she sensitively and effectively integrate her own unique qualities with those of her followers and with the objectives of the organization. Such an awareness enhances a leader's ability to direct work activities. For instance, when conflict arises, the leader can use her knowledge of the people involved to seek the best resolution. When groups form to accomplish a task, the leader can capitalize on her knowledge of the members' skills and attitudes.

Chart #6 outlines the various interpersonal activities leaders

6 HUMAN RELATIONS SKILLS

	First-line/Low	Middle	Top	Executive
Intragroup relations	• Is aware of own attitudes, assumptions and beliefs about other individuals • Knows about how groups work and about human behavior • Develops a work environment that is supportive and involves participation by all • Shows continual interest in employees' needs and problems and responds appropriately • Facilitates resolution of conflict in work unit	• Establishes programs to help emphasize appreciation of others' values, attitudes, and beliefs • Applies knowledge of group dynamics and human behavior • Resolves interpersonal and interunit conflicts	• Works to create supportive work environment • Sets up and conducts meetings	• Develops policy endorsing diversity of personnel
Intergroup relations	• Interprets and applies goals of organization to work group • Reports needs of subordinates to middle management	• Plans intergroup relations • Integrates individual's needs with those of organization	• Formulates policy that integrates varying group interests and activities • Creates supportive organizational climate	• Endorses policy • Represents the organization with external groups

pursue at different levels in the organization. Note that the chart includes intragroup relations—those occurring within a group or work unit—and intergroup relations—those occurring between groups and units or between organizations.

As you read across the chart, you will get an idea of the types of activities and knowledge utilized by leaders at all levels. Notice that those in first-line and low-level supervisory positions expend the most energy in intragroup relations. Because they must maximize the collaborative efforts of the work group, they need good human relations skills in their frequent and direct contact. The middle managers play a dual role in understanding those above and below them. At this level, leaders apply their knowledge of human behavior and group dynamics in an effort to create an environment conducive to productive and satisfying work relationships. Their proximity to workers warrants a knowledge of human relations, but there is less need for daily application of the skills. Top managers are expected to have integrated human relations skills into their style and to have trained their subordinates in them. The human relations role of the executive is to determine policies that will improve the organization's climate and procedures.

As you continue reading through the chart, notice that responsibility for intergroup relations falls primarily on leaders at the middle and higher levels of the organization. These leaders need to be aware of what is happening in the total organization rather than in only one unit. They must develop policies and programs that enhance the relationships between work units and between the organization and outside groups.

Evaluate your own organization in terms of these responsibilities. Are they similar? Different? How?

Assessing Your Human Relations Skills

You are now ready to assess your own human relations skills. First, decide whether you want to focus on improving skills for your current leadership position or on developing skills for the level above you. Then review chart **#6** to determine the skills you already possess. Rate these strengths with the following code:

+3   Highly developed
+2   Somewhat developed
+1   Minimally developed

For instance, if you've had considerable experience in developing and maintaining a supportive work environment, you might rate yourself a +2 or +3.

Next, review the chart to identify those skills you'd like to develop more fully. Use a similar rating system:

> −1   Needs minimal development
> −2   Needs some development
> −3   Needs considerable development

For instance, if you have had many interpersonal conflicts but do not feel you have been successful in resolving them, you might rate yourself −2.

List the skills that need the most development on the planning sheet in chart **#7,** under the column marked "Skills I want to develop." Number those listed in the order in which you want to develop them. Now you can plan to meet these specific needs.

This chapter covers the following human relations topics:

1. *Working in and with groups.* How can you set up and run more effective meetings? What roles are played by people when they are in groups? Which do you play? How can you increase the number of roles played by members?
2. *Your style and choices in conflict.* What is your style of dealing with conflict? What are some methods of dealing with conflict? What is the impact of a win-win, win-lose, and lose-lose stance on you and others?

On your planning sheet, check the skills you want to develop that are covered in this chapter and write down any additional resources (books, organizations, people) to help you meet your needs. Remember to check the resources section at the end of this chapter for additional ideas.

Working In and With Groups

Working with and in groups is an integral part of leadership. Think about the past two weeks and make a list of all the groups in which you were included. A quick look at your calendar should provide you with this information. Were you a leader or a participant? What activities did the group engage in? For example, the group may have:

> Exchanged information.
> Solved a problem.

7   PLANNING SHEET FOR SKILLS IN HUMAN RELATIONS

Skills I want to develop	Order of development	Found in chapter	Additional resources

Supported group members.

Made a decision.

Talked about many topics without reaching a resolution.

Focusing on your role as both a participant and a leader can help you understand group dynamics. When you reflect on your own experience, you can diagnose effective and ineffective behaviors and thus improve your leadership skills with groups.

This section focuses on groups formed to share information, solve problems, make decisions, and accomplish tasks. The following topics are examined.

1. How to make the necessary arrangements for a meeting.
2. How to set up an agenda and establish the tone of the meeting.
3. How to identify both helpful and hindering roles in meetings and groups.
4. How to assess the group roles that women usually play and to determine which additional roles would make them more effective as leaders.

Arranging meetings

When you assume responsibility for planning small or large meetings, you become involved in several tasks. These can be grouped into seven categories: program or agenda, arrangements, materials, fiscal activities, evaluation, publicity, and registration.

To hold a successful meeting, you must deal with each of these tasks. While you can and should delegate tasks to others (as outlined in the following chapter on supervision), it is important that you as the planner have an overview of the process. Often the number of tasks involved and the need to complete them within a limited time can seem overwhelming, but with careful planning, you can reduce both anxiety and mistakes.

Use the guide for planning a meeting (#8) to help you organize. Tasks are arranged in roughly chronological order, based on other leaders' experience in planning meetings. If your organization has different procedures, you may need to rearrange the sequence of tasks. The guide is comprehensive enough to include steps for a meeting that requires such details as registration and displays. If the meeting you are planning is not as complex, ignore the tasks that do not pertain.

As you identify who will be responsible for each task, write the person's initials under the column marked "Who." Use the column marked "Started on" to indicate the date you began a particular task. As each task is completed, note the date in the column marked "Completed on." These two columns give you an at-a-glance view of what has been done, what is in progress, and what is next.

Preparing an agenda

An agenda is a list of items to be covered in a meeting. It organizes and guides the direction of the meeting. Have you ever attended a meeting in which an agenda was not prepared or followed? You can probably recall your frustration and irritation over wasted time. The proper use of agendas, then, is an essential skill for leaders.

To prepare an agenda, consider each item to be covered, the person presenting it, the type of interaction involved, and the time needed. Example #9 outlines a proposed agenda for a staff meeting.

There are three basic types of agendas: closed, open, and evolving. In order to choose the most appropriate type (or combination), you must be clear on the purpose of the meeting, the readiness of group members to follow a particular type of agenda (some members may be so unfamiliar with using agendas that a progression from closed to evolving to open is warranted), and the amount of time available.

THE CLOSED AGENDA

In a closed agenda, items to be dealt with at a meeting are listed in advance of the discussion. There is no opportunity to alter the agenda during the meeting. A closed agenda is appropriate when the planner knows that certain items must be dealt with at a particular meeting. You should develop the agenda well before the meeting, allowing yourself time to define the purpose and objectives of the meeting and to uncover problems or information that need to be discussed. Solicit ideas on potential agenda items from your followers. Ask them to report items of concern to you in advance of the meeting and make a file for these items as they emerge. Once you have collected them, organize the agenda items into a sequence for introduction and action.

Send the proposed agenda to participants well in advance of the meeting to be sure they understand the time, location, purpose, and objectives of the meeting and are aware of the information to be conveyed, the problems to be discussed, and their responsibilities as participants. The more prepared everyone is, the more likely the meeting will be successful.

THE OPEN AGENDA

In this type, items for consideration are suggested *at* the meeting. The open agenda works well when a group meets regularly, is willing to follow this type of agenda, and has time to develop it at the beginning of each meeting. The following steps are involved in building an open agenda:

1. Each person suggests items for the agenda.
2. The items are posted on a chart or chalkboard, with the initials of the individual introducing the item and the approximate amount of time needed.
3. An open discussion is held to clarify the purpose of each item.
4. Items are grouped into homogeneous clusters.
5. Group members express their priorities for attending to these items.
6. The final agenda is rewritten and posted.

THE EVOLVING AGENDA

The evolving agenda utilizes elements of both the closed and open methods. The meeting planner collects items for discussion and presentation and posts them in advance or at the beginning of the meeting. Group members offer suggestions and discuss priorities for allocating meeting time. If other important topics emerge during the meeting, the group can stop discussion and decide if the agenda needs to be reordered to allow for the additional items.

STICK TO THE AGENDA

Once an agenda has been prepared, whether in advance of the meeting or on the spot, it is important that you stick to it. Your agenda is an agreement about the use of time and the responsibilities of participants. Meetings will be more productive and participants more involved and committed when the agenda is observed. At times, you may have to monitor the discussion carefully to make sure the agenda is followed, interrupting when the direction wavers or excessive time is spent on an item.

You may want to assign one of the participants as a timekeeper to let the group know when the allotted time is over. The group (or leader) can then determine if more time should be allowed. Another way to make sure the agenda is followed is to assign a process observer to keep a record of the roles people are playing in the group (see the section on group roles later in the chapter). Rotate these assignments among the members to give all participants an opportunity to learn more about group roles and group dynamics.

Poorly planned meetings

Poorly planned meetings are a waste of time and energy. Your time is valuable and must be used wisely. Perhaps you can identify with one

8   GUIDE FOR PLANNING A MEETING

Tasks prior to meeting	Who	Started on	Com- pleted on
1. Determine goals and objectives of meeting	___	___	___
2. Determine tasks to be accomplished and person responsible	___	___	___
3. Prepare budget	___	___	___
4. List alternative dates for meeting	___	___	___
5. List and contact alternative sites for meeting	___	___	___
6. Select best date and time	___	___	___
7. Select site; confirm arrangements in writing	___	___	___
8. Prepare first draft of meeting agenda	___	___	___
9. Identify, review, and select people needed for meeting's program	___	___	___
10. Contact resource people and confirm arrangements in writing	___	___	___
11. Prepare and send advance publicity on meeting date, site, and agenda	___	___	___
12. List and arrange for supplies and audio-visual equipment needed	___	___	___
13. Gather and duplicate printed materials needed for meeting	___	___	___
14. Arrange for displays or other materials needed	___	___	___
15. Send follow-up publicity notice or reminders	___	___	___
16. Prepare and duplicate final agenda	___	___	___
17. Prepare and duplicate evaluation form	___	___	___
18. Process advance registrations	___	___	___
19. Confirm arrangements at meeting site for date, times, room setups, equipment and supplies, beverages, and food	___	___	___
20. Prepare signs needed	___	___	___
21. Arrange for additional personnel to assist with registration, hosting, program, audio-visual presentations	___	___	___
Tasks on day of meeting	___	___	___
22. Arrange for packing and delivery of all materials, supplies, and equipment	___	___	___
23. Double-check all site arrangements	___	___	___

8   GUIDE FOR PLANNING A MEETING (Continued)

Tasks on day of meeting	Who	Started on	Completed on
24. Supervise setup of displays, signs, and registration			
25. Greet and register meeting participants; collect any monies			
26. Check that all arrangements go as instructed; solve problems as they arise			
27. Distribute and collect evaluations			
Tasks following meeting			
28. Pack supplies, equipment, and materials			
29. Collect and pay any bills			
30. Arrange for proper return of supplies, equipment, and materials			
31. Review evaluations of meeting and note recommendations			
32. Prepare follow-up report or minutes to be filed or sent to participants			
33. Send letters of appreciation to those who helped arrange for or participated in the program			

9   FORMAT FOR A PROPOSED AGENDA

Staff meeting for April 1978 (Chair: Renee)   9:00–10:00 A.M.

Agenda item	Person presenting	Type of interaction	Estimated time needed
1. Minutes of last meeting	Tom	Information given for approval	5 min.
2. Update on plans for publicity for executive training program	Carlos	Information sharing	15 min.
3. Review of needs assessment of technical staff and recommendations	Dolores	Information sharing and discussion	35 min.
4. Dates and times for staff meetings for next quarter	Renee	Participation	5 min.

woman executive who attended a high-level meeting that began at 11:00 A.M. At 4:30 P.M. she stood up and announced that she was leaving and that if the group couldn't make any decision by 4:30 it wasn't likely to by 8:00 P.M.!

You may not want to be as direct in expressing your dissatisfaction with the progress of a meeting, but you need not passively endure an unproductive meeting while secretly glancing at your watch. Consider the following alternatives.

1. If an agenda doesn't exist, ask for one. Before you go into a meeting, be clear about its purpose and time demands.

2. Insist that the meeting start on time out of respect for those who made the effort to be there promptly.

3. If you are unclear about the items on a published agenda, ask for clarification at the start of the meeting.

4. Hold the group members and leader accountable. If they indicate that there will be a 30-minute discussion on one item and 35 minutes have passed, speak up. You might say, "I want to point out that we have passed the time limit allotted to this item. I suggest that we call for a vote."

5. When fatigue sets in, productivity drops, so ask for a stretch or a break. Others most likely feel the same way and will appreciate your expressing this need.

6. Weigh the advantages and disadvantages of leaving a meeting that far exceeds its time limit. Your leaving may remind others that everyone's time is valuable or it may create hostility toward you.

Establishing a productive meeting climate

As the leader in a meeting, you are responsible for creating a climate conducive to productivity. If you reflect on successful and unsuccessful meetings you have attended, you can recognize some of the variables involved. As you set the tone for your meetings, consider the following questions:

1. How important do participants perceive the meeting to be? If they consider the meeting's purpose and their presence important (and if they perceive those in attendance as prestigious), participants will be more motivated to attend. If group members feel that their presence is not important, motivation to attend will drop. It is your job to reverse this attitude and make each person feel important and needed at each meeting.

2. Is the overall atmosphere competitive or cooperative? If members perceive the atmosphere to be competitive and evaluative, interpersonal interactions may be restricted and important information

withheld. A collaborative atmosphere is conducive to increased interaction and development.

3. What is the size of the group? It is easier for people to get to know one another and to develop a sense of unity in a smaller group. It is more difficult to communicate and become involved in larger groups. Thus on certain occasions you may want to form smaller work units within the total group.

4. Where is the meeting to be held? How close is the location of the meeting to those attending? How attractive and comfortable is the site? Does it minimize interruptions during the meeting? Where you hold a meeting can affect its success. Dark, cheerless, uncomfortable rooms are deterrents to creativity.

5. When is the meeting to be held? The choice of time is crucial. Planning a meeting when people are fatigued from a day's or week's work is unproductive.

6. How will members participate in the meeting? Are they to participate in planning the agenda and making decisions? Are they only to receive information? Are they to make rubber-stamp decisions? To avoid confusion and frustration, make sure all members are clear about their involvement.

7. What roles are to be assigned or taken? Are they clear? Are they acceptable to participants? (The various roles that occur in groups and ways to utilize them productively are discussed in the next section.)

8. What process is to be used to make decisions? Is this process known to group members? How comfortable are they with it? The clearer the process, the more prepared everyone will be to tackle problems.

9. Are support and challenge to be balanced in the meeting? Excessive challenge and criticism create a climate of defensiveness that inhibits the involvement of participants. Excessive support can also be inappropriate, especially when pertinent, constructive criticisms are needed to solve a problem. It is important to provide a balance of the two in your meeting.

Roles people play in a group

As a leader, it is important that you understand the basic principles of group dynamics, particularly the roles that people play in groups. A role is defined as a set of behaviors displayed by an individual. Sometimes an individual consistently assumes a particular role; at other times the individual alternates among several roles, depending on her or his mood or intention. For instance, the person who announces, "I'm just playing devil's advocate," is intentionally and temporarily taking an opposing position—that is, assuming a role.

10a   TASK ROLES

Helping

Arranger: prepares setup of room; passes out materials and refreshments; operates equipment.

Clarifier: interprets ideas and suggestions; clears up confusion; indicates alternatives and issues before the group; gives examples; defines terms.

Consensus taker: checks with group to see how much agreement has been reached and how ready the members are to consider a decision.

Information or opinion giver: offers facts; provides relevant information about group concerns; states a belief; gives suggestions, ideas, or opinions.

Information or opinion seeker: requests facts; seeks relevant information about a group concern; asks for suggestions, ideas, or opinions.

Initiator: proposes task or goals; defines a group problem; suggests procedure or ideas for getting the task accomplished.

Navigator: keeps group members on the agenda or task; draws attention when the group goes off course.

Recorder: writes down suggestions; makes a record of group decisions.

Summarizer: pulls together related ideas; restates suggestions after group has discussed them; offers a decision or conclusion for the group to accept or reject.

Hindering

Avoider: remains oblivious to the task or problem; shows no interest in seeking additional information.

Decider: without checking with the group, decides that enough discussion has taken place to reach a decision; values efficiency and speed in deliberation.

Ignorer: remains unaware of or unconcerned about confusion of others; ignores any disagreements and doesn't seek to clarify anything that might lead to conflict.

Mover: charges ahead before checking for readiness to summarize or closure.

Playboy-playgirl: regards the meeting as a social occasion; jokes and pokes fun at other members; helps everyone have a "good time."

Talker: engages in excessive talking about her own ideas; interrupts others.

Waiter: waits for others to initiate action, offer opinions or facts; answers when asked.

Roles can be grouped into two types: task and maintenance. Task roles focus on the job or task to be done; maintenance roles focus on relationships among members of the group. While both types may operate at the same time in a group, one may dominate the other.

Charts #**10a** and **10b** identify some task and maintenance roles, grouped according to whether they have the potential to hinder a group's progress. As you read the various descriptions, identify the roles you *generally* take in group settings, both as a participant and as a leader.

APPROPRIATE LEADERSHIP ROLES

The role you play as a leader in meetings depends entirely on the task before the group and the readiness, experience, and motivation of

10b   MAINTENANCE ROLES

Helping

Compromiser: when her own idea or position is at stake in a conflict, offers a compromise in which she may lose status; admits error; modifies her position in the interest of group cohesiveness or growth.

Encourager: is friendly, warm, and responsive to others; accepts others and their contributions; shows regard for others by giving them recognition or an opportunity to contribute.

Feeler: expresses group feelings; senses moods and relationships within the group; shares own feelings with other members.

Gatekeeper: helps to keep communication channels open; facilitates the participation of others; suggests procedures that permit sharing.

Group process observer: keeps watch on how the group is functioning and what helpful and hindering roles are used; periodically gives a report on observations.

Harmonizer: attempts to reconcile disagreements; reduces tension; helps people explore their differences.

Standard setter and tester: checks whether the group is satisfied with its procedures; suggests new procedures when necessary.

Hindering

Blocker: disagrees and opposes beyond reason; stubbornly resists the group's wishes for personal reasons; uses hidden agenda to thwart group progress.

Caucus former: seeks out one or more supporters to promote her special needs regardless of the group's wishes.

Challenger: incites conflicts among members; "needles" and irritates others; uses emotionally charged words and sarcasm; puts down others' ideas.

Cold-shoulderer: is unresponsive and unfriendly toward others; generally ignores contributions of members.

Conformist: always agrees with whatever the group wants; smooths over any conflict.

Emoter: expresses a feeling about every idea, suggestion, or problem, usually with a great deal of emotion; tries to psychoanalyze others and unveil their feelings.

---

its members. In other words, your role depends on the situation. (A complete discussion of situational leadership is found in Chapter 5.) If, for example, group members are unfamiliar with one another and with the purpose of the meeting, the leader needs to assume an initiator role. If the group is floundering or if time is at a premium, an initiator role is again appropriate. If, however, some group members are thoroughly familiar with the goals and objectives of the meeting and are highly motivated, the leader should assume the role of encourager, fostering initiative in others. If individuals with experience or knowledge of the topic are reluctant to contribute, an encourager role is again appropriate. Obviously, a leader does not play one role throughout a meeting. Rather, the leader is alert to roles that need to be played during the meeting and adopts these roles as required to ensure that the task is accomplished and group harmony maintained.

PROBLEMS IN ROLE PLAYING

There are four major problems that can arise when people interact in groups: stereotypic sex-role behavior, overuse of roles, underuse of roles, and inappropriate use of roles.

Stereotypic sex-role behavior. Both men and women can easily fall into stereotypic sex-role behavior. Both sexes have learned particular patterns of working in groups and tend to adopt certain roles over others. Review the task and maintenance roles chart and identify the roles you think are most commonly adopted by women and men. Your list may include many of the following:

		Women	*Men*
Maintenance			
	Helpful	Encourager, harmonizer, feeler, gatekeeper, compromiser	Compromiser
	Hindering	Conformist, emoter	Challenger, blocker, caucus former
Task			
	Helpful	Information or opinion seeker, clarifier, recorder, arranger	Initiator, information or opinion giver, summarizer
	Hindering	Waiter, avoider, withdrawer, ignorer	Talker, mover, ignorer, decider

Men generally adopt active task roles and focus on developing their own ideas and opinions, while women use task roles that are helpful to others. In addition, women assume more maintenance roles than men. These sex-typed roles are developed in childhood and are continuously reinforced by the schools, the media, and the expectations of others. However, such inflexible role patterns do not lead to effective leadership and maximum participation in group situations. Both men and women, then, should strive to become more flexible, to increase the range of roles they are able to play, and to use them as they fit the situation.

Overuse of roles. A second problem that often arises in group interactions is the overuse of roles, particularly the information or opinion giver, talker, waiter, challenger, blocker, and conformist, which have the potential to hinder the group's progress.

Overuse of the *information or opinion giver* and *talker* roles can result in one person's dominating the group. Men often create this problem by talking on and on about the topic at hand or about extraneous items. If interrupted, they may maneuver the focus back to them in order to continue talking. It is important for the leader to stop the talker (women can be talkers too), or only a few members will be heard.

Overuse of the *waiter* role can play into the hands of the talker. Because many women lack confidence in the value of their contributions or in their right to express opinions and ideas, they tend to sit back and listen to others rather than initiate ideas or solutions. The waiter waits to be asked and frequently hopes that she isn't called upon to speak. An astute leader will identify the waiters and provide the encouragement and structure needed to ensure their participation in a meeting.

A variety of shared-time techniques are available to you as a leader to deal with those who talk excessively, give out too much information, or wait:

1. Make it a rule that, for each topic being discussed, every participant must say something before another person can give a second opinion.

2. Determine a time limit for presentations of ideas or opinions. Use a bell or timer to monitor each speaker.

3. If you feel that a person has taken ample time or has begun to digress, interrupt and say so. Do it clearly and firmly and as often as necessary.

Overuse of the *challenger* and *blocker* roles—usually by men—undermines the group's interests and disrupts group harmony. Men's style of communication incorporates an element of challenge. Men tend to ask "why" questions more often than women. Such questions, as noted earlier, often put the respondent on the defensive. The section on conflict in this chapter suggests ways to deal with this problem.

The blocker, whose primary concern is the pursuit of her or his own interests, disregards the direction of the group and threatens group harmony. The attitude is one of "I intend to get my own say." The rights of individual expression override group decision making.

The leader will need to be firm with the blocker to prevent that person from interrupting the progress of the group. The use of the three techniques listed above should keep the blocker from dominating the meeting.

Overuse of the *conformist* and *ignorer* roles—common among women—can thwart the group's efforts to resolve a conflict. Conformists tend to deny the value of their ideas and opinions and quickly agree to whatever the group or leader suggest. Ignorers too will agree to anything in order to avoid conflict. It is the leader's responsibility to assist the ignorer and conformist so that problems are dealt with, rather than ignored or avoided. This can be done by affirming the value of each person's contributions, by applying the suggestions given in the next section ("Learning from Conflict"), and by using shared-time techniques.

Underuse of roles. A third problem that can arise in group settings is the underuse of certain roles, particularly the feeler role for men and the initiator, information or opinion giver, summarizer, and navigator roles for women.

Underuse of the *feeler* role prevents group members from knowing how each person feels about the tasks at hand, the organization, and those in it. Men have been socialized to withhold expressions of feeling, especially those revealing tenderness or vulnerability. Authors such as Goldberg, Farrell, and Chesler (see the resources section) can help you understand the sources and implications of men's socializing patterns. The leader who understands the underlying cause of men's reticence to express feelings has taken the first step toward overcoming its negative effects. A sensitive leader can listen for clues about the emotions behind a man's words and encourage their expression. The communication skills presented in Chapter 3 may be useful with this problem.

Underuse of the *initiator, information* and *opinion giver, summarizer,* and *navigator* roles may lead the group to flounder in its direction and purpose. Women need to learn to assert their basic right to present ideas and opinions to others. The readings on assertiveness training listed in the resources section are useful tools for overcoming this problem.

Inappropriate use of roles. The fourth problem that often arises in group interactions is the inappropriate use of roles, particularly those of harmonizer, mover, decider, and feeler.

The *harmonizer* role can be useful when conflict needs to be smoothed over, especially when there is not enough time to resolve a problem or when the group is not really ready to deal with it. Women, however, tend to misuse this role by interrupting conflict prematurely because of their desire to avoid disruption. The wise leader learns to assess when harmonizing behaviors are appropriate to the situation.

Movers and *deciders* are potentially hindering unless their use is appropriately timed. A mover decides the group has discussed the topic enough and is ready for a decision or closure. While she or he may be ready, the group may not be, and attempts to move the group faster can cause resentment and confusion. A decider tends to be overly anxious to finish the talk at hand and becomes restless when she or he thinks enough time has been spent talking. Although attention to time, decision making, and adherence to the agenda is valuable, overconcern with these items is just as inappropriate as lack of concern.

The *feeler* role is valuable to groups, but both men and women can use it inappropriately if they overexpress their feelings. Women often do this by crying, which leaves other members confused and at a loss. Although some people think crying puts women at an advantage, it doesn't. A one-up/one-down relationship is never advantageous. Men tend to overexpress their feelings through anger, which is also inappropriate. It is the leader's responsibility to watch for feelings as they emerge. Expression of feelings needs to be encouraged, but the leader should intervene when such expression is inappropriate. Call a break. Table the topic until a later time. Request that parties with strong emotional reactions to a topic meet with you privately (separately or together). Allow for the expression of feelings, but never at a time or in a place in which an individual will come out a loser.

THE LEADER'S GOAL

As an effective leader, your goal is to increase the use of helpful task and maintenance roles and to decrease the use of hindering roles in both yourself and others. How do you reach this goal? First, identify your own style of group behavior. What helpful and hindering roles do you consistently use? Which do you overuse? Monitor yourself and make a conscious effort not to overuse these roles. Which roles do you underuse? Make it an objective to adopt them more often. Begin utilizing more of your talents. Ask group members for feedback on your progress and for reminders when you slip from your stated objective.

Second, teach those in your work group about task and maintenance roles. Encourage them to increase their repertoire of helpful roles and to decrease their repertoire of hindering roles. Suggest, for example, that the roles of navigator and group process observer be rotated. The person serving as the group process observer can use chart #11 to record her perceptions of the roles assumed by members of the group and to report what she has observed. It is especially important that the process observer not *evaluate* what occurs, but merely *describe*.

Working in and with groups can be productive and meaningful to everyone involved. The leader who pays careful attention to the administrative details of setting up meetings, planning the most appropriate agenda, and working to increase the number of helpful task and maintenance roles played by group members will be successful.

Learning from Conflict

Conflict is a part of life that cannot—and in fact should not—always be avoided. Conflict can be healthy when it is used to clarify expectations, needs, and roles and to strengthen relationships. Understanding and dealing with conflict is an important skill for leaders at all levels of an organization.

As indicated on the human relations chart (#6) at the beginning of this chapter, leaders at the lower and middle levels of the organization need skills for dealing with intragroup conflicts, while those at the

11   RECORD OF TASK AND MAINTENANCE ROLES

Directions to group observer:

As you observe the task and maintenance roles that emerge in the group, record your observations. List the roles in the left-hand column. Place the names of group members along the top of the page. Use tally marks to keep track of the number of times each behavior is observed.

Task roles				
1.				
2.				
3.				
4.				
5.				
6.				
Maintenance roles				
1.				
2.				
3.				
4.				
5.				
6.				

12   APPROACHES TO DEALING WITH CONFLICT

Type	Behavior	Favorite phrases
Soldier	Fights back	"Oh yeah?" "Sez who?"
Abdicator	Agrees with other person; takes the blame	"You're right, I did that wrong."
Apologizer	Expresses regret	"I'm sorry."
Defender	Justifies and defends position	"Let me explain." "Yes, but. . . ." "You don't understand."
Feeler	Expresses feelings	"When you do that, I feel. . . ." "I'm feeling. . . ."
Negotiator	Tries to find a compromise	"Let's talk this over so we can find a solution."
God	Dictates the resolution	"Of course I'm right." "Do it my way."
Avoider	Smooths over conflict; avoids it at all costs	"This is nothing to fight over." "Let's forget it."

upper levels need skills for dealing with intergroup conflicts. This section helps you determine your approach to dealing with conflict and reviews several methods for resolving conflict with a win-win philosophy.

The first step in understanding how to resolve conflict is to clarify your own attitude toward it. What is your reaction when you observe a conflict between two people? Fear? Excitement? Anxiety? How do you react when you have a conflict with a subordinate? With a colleague? With a superior?

Your attitude stems in part from the lessons or "messages" you learned from others about conflict. Make a list of messages you received from your parents, school, church, and culture. Which of them do you still believe in and adhere to today? Do any of those listed below apply to your attitudes toward conflict?

"Girls don't fight."
"Don't pick a fight; but if you're in one, win it."
"Fighting never settled anything."
"Children should not see their parents fight."
"If you can't say something nice, don't say anything at all."
"Turn the other cheek."
"An eye for an eye."

Identifying your style of dealing with conflict

Chart **#12** outlines eight different approaches to dealing with conflict. Review it and identify those that best describe your conflict "style." Think about conflicts you have had with others in the past. Analyzing them can give you further clues to your basic style.

Next, choose at least four of the people listed in chart **#13** and describe a recent conflict you have had with each one. In the column labeled "Causes of conflict" make a few notes on the nature of conflict so you can explore it. Then recall what both you and the other party did in the situation. What approach did each of you use? Use key words from chart **#12** to describe the differences. For example: "I apologized." "She defended." Finally, think about the conflict in terms of winning and losing. Who won? Who lost? Did you both win? Both lose? If you won the argument but strained the relationship, you both lost.

Now look at your chart for patterns. Compare the information within the columns for similarities and differences. For instance, are there similarities in the causes of your conflicts? With which people do you have the most conflict?

CAUSES OF CONFLICT

The first step in resolving a conflict is to clearly and thoroughly identify the problem and its source. Therefore, when you are involved in conflict, analyze the situation. There are several basic, recurring causes of conflict:

Values. Conflict can arise over different values. Everyone has certain values or attitudes toward money, relationships, friends, politics, health, sex, work, race, gender, and age. These values develop throughout a person's lifetime, and are sometimes reinforced and sometimes changed by new experiences. A person's values shape her or his basic position toward other people and toward the world. The strength of such a position is based on the many feelings invested in it. Therefore, when a conflict concerns a value, it is very difficult to change a person's position. A wiser approach is to try to clarify the value at issue, understand its importance to the other person, and accept that person's position. The values clarification process originated by Raths, Harmin, and Simon (see the resources section) is a useful tool for achieving this goal.

Perception. Conflict also occurs when those involved "see" the situation or "hear" accounts differently. As described more fully in Chapter 3, perceptions are based on individual needs, wants, attitudes, and values. What is perceived feels very real to each person, and even basic perceptions of what the conflict is about can differ. Sentences that

13 CONFLICT CHART

Person	Causes of conflict	Approach used		Who won?			
		By me	By other party	I did	Other did	Both won	Both lost
Stranger							
Acquaintance							
Close friend							
Spouse or partner							
Boss							
Colleague							
Subordinate							
Client							
Own child							
Own parent							
Other							

begin with "I see" or "I heard" are clues that the cause of conflict may
be a difference in perception.

Expectations. Conflict often arises over different expectations. For
instance, Ann expects others to tell her when her work is not
satisfactory, whereas her boss expects Ann to ask for feedback on her
job performance. Both wait for something to happen until one of them
does not fulfill the other's expectations, and conflict emerges. Phrases
such as "I expected you to" and "I wanted you to" are clues that
expectations are the basis for the conflict.

Roles. Many conflicts occur when roles are not clearly defined. For
example, you may find, as the new person in a position, that appropriate roles are entirely clear, or you may choose to develop your own
approach to the job. Yet those around you may remember how your
predecessor fulfilled that role and make judgments accordingly. You
might hear, "Joe never did it that way," or "We've always done it like
this."

Power. Conflict can occur around power issues. Power can be either
real or perceived. A person in a position of authority should have real
power because her role grants her the authority to provide or withhold
resources such as money, materials, time, and information. A conflict
may occur when that person doesn't exercise her authority. Others may
perceive her to have power that she doesn't think she has. Of course,
the opposite can also occur—and often does with women leaders. She
may hold the title to a position that, on paper, is powerful; yet those
above her and below her may ignore or discount her authority.

Return to your conflict chart and determine the source or sources
of each conflict you have listed. Did it arise over a difference in values
or perceptions, a lack of clarity about expectations or roles, or a power
issue? Each conflict is likely to have more than one cause.

With Whom Do You Have Conflicts?

With which people do you generally have conflicts? Are they those
with whom you are more intimate (spouse, parents, children, loved
ones) or less intimate (acquaintances, colleagues)? Do conflicts arise
more often when you have authority or power over others or when
others have that over you? Do you have more conflicts with women or
with men? Do you have conflicts more or less often with people of a
different race, religion, or ethnic background?

As you analyze your answers to these questions, you may find
certain patterns emerging. If your conflicts do not fall into clear
patterns, you can treat each case individually. However, if you consistently have conflicts with the same type of people, such as those who
have authority over you, you need to explore more fully why that
happens. If any one pattern causes you a great deal of anxiety or

requires considerable energy to resolve, you may want to seek counseling to find a healthier balance in your life.

Methods of resolving conflict

Looking again at your conflict chart, count the different methods you used to resolve the conflicts listed. Review the eight approaches to dealing with conflict for clues. How extensive was your repertoire of methods? What methods were used by others involved in the conflicts?

Keeping in mind your own and others' styles, study the method for resolving conflict listed in chart #14. Each of these methods is appropriate in certain circumstances. As suggested throughout this book, it is crucial for leaders to select behaviors appropriate to a given situation. Thus, before you choose a method for resolving a conflict, analyze the problem thoroughly. What is happening? What is the attitude of those involved? How much time is available? Have the parties agreed to the same method? Are those involved knowledgeable in and comfortable with the method?

As you can see, basic to conflict resolution are skills in communication, decision making, running meetings, and problem solving, all of which are discussed elsewhere in this book.

The most effective method of resolving conflict is one that enables both parties to win. This means that each person is satisfied with the outcome, her or his morale is high, and relationships remain good. When either or both parties have negative feelings about the outcome, resentments can build until they later explode. While successfully presenting an argument or a point is often thought to be winning, a deeper look often reveals a loss as well—perhaps in the quality of the relationship involved. Trust may be lessened or destroyed. All those involved are the losers.

Effective leaders seek a win-win approach as often as possible. Although it can be difficult to achieve and requires considerable time and effort, the results are worthwhile. Effective leaders also understand that a win-win approach is not always feasible. Thus the wise leader assesses the situation carefully, clarifies the problem thoroughly, and chooses the most appropriate method.

Women's and men's view of conflict

Women tend to adopt a win-win philosophy more often than men in their interactions. They have been socialized to consider others' needs and wishes and to seek ways to accommodate other people's positions. Men have been socialized to compete with others and to strive to win. This basic difference can be observed during a game: Men will

14 METHODS FOR RESOLVING CONFLICT

Method	Results	Appropriate	Inappropriate	Skills required
Denial or withdrawal	Person tries to solve problem by denying its existence; results in win–lose	When issue is relatively unimportant; when issue is raised at inopportune time	When issue is important; when it will not disappear, but will build to greater complexity	Judgment of what is needed in the situation
Suppression or smoothing over	Differences are played down; results in win–lose	Same as above; also when preservation of relationship is more important than issue	When evasion of issue will disrupt relationship; when others are ready and willing to deal with issue	Empathy
Power or dominance	Authority, position, majority rule, or a persuasive minority settles the conflict; results in win–lose	When authority is granted by one's position; also when group has agreed on method of decision-making	When those without power have no means to express their needs and ideas, especially if this lack of opportunity has the potential of future disruption	Decision making; running effective meetings
Compromise or negotiation	Each party gives up something in order to meet midway; results in some loss of each side's position	When both sides have enough leeway to give; when resources are limited; when win–lose stance is undesirable	When original position is inflated or unrealistic; when solution must be watered down to be acceptable; when commitment by both parties is doubtful	Attentive listening and paraphrasing; problem solving
Collaboration	Individual abilities and expertise are recognized; each person's position is clear, but emphasis is on group solution; results in win–win	When time is available to complete process; when parties are committed to and trained in use of process	When time is limited; when parties lack training in or commitment to collaborative efforts	Attentive listening and paraphrasing; problem solving

generally be most interested in winning, while women will be most interested in how the game is played!

As noted earlier, however, women's tendency to accommodate others and to smooth over incidents is not always beneficial. Women need to be careful about withdrawing or smoothing over conflict in situations where resolution is essential. In addition, women need to develop their negotiation skills so they can enlarge their repertoire of methods for resolving conflict.

Conflict can be healthy or harmful, meaningful or meaningless. It is up to you as a leader to use conflict positively—and to teach your followers to use it positively—so that tasks are accomplished and good human relations maintained. Remember this equation:

Effectiveness = Accomplishment of Tasks
+ Maintenance of Good Human Relations

Although many human relations skills are essential for effective leadership, the two presented in this chapter form the core. Learning and applying knowledge about group dynamics and conflict solving will increase the likelihood that tasks will get done *and* that morale will be high.

RESOURCES

Assertiveness

Alberti, Robert, and Michael Emmons. *Your Perfect Right: A Guide to Assertive Behavior*. San Luis Obispo, CA: Impact Publishers, 1974.

Bach, George, and Herb Goldberg. *Creative Aggression: The Art of Assertive Living*. New York: Avon Books, 1974.

Bloom, Lynn Z., Daren Coburn, and Joan Perelman. *The New Assertive Woman*. New York: Dell, 1975.

James, Muriel, and Dorothy Jongeward. *Born to Win*. New York: Signet Books, 1978.

Jongeward, Dorothy, and Dru Scott. *Women as Winners*. Reading, MA: Addison-Wesley, 1976.

Phelps, Stanley, and Linda Austin. *The Assertive Woman*. San Luis Obispo, CA: Impact Publishers, 1970.

Conflict and Values

Filley, Alan. *Interpersonal Conflict*. La Jolla, CA: University Associates, 1975.

Kirschenbaum, Howard. *Advanced Values Clarification*, 1975. Available from National Humanistic Center, 110 Spring Street, Saratoga Springs, NY 12866.

Likert, Rensis, and Jane Gibson Likert. *New Ways of Handling Conflict*. La Jolla, CA: University Associates, 1976.

Raths, Louis, Merrill Harmin, and Sidney Simon. *Values and Teaching*. Columbus, OH: Charles Merrill, 1966.

Simon, Sidney. *Negative Criticism*. Niles, IL: Argus Communications, 1978.

Groups and Meetings

Bradford, Leland. *Making Meetings Work: A Guide for Leaders and Group Members.* La Jolla, CA: University Associates, 1976.

Cohen, Arthur, and Douglas Smith. *The Critical Incident in Growth Groups.* La Jolla, CA: University Associates, 1976.

Doyle, Michael, and David Straus. *How to Make Meetings Work.* Chicago: Playboy Press, 1976.

Dunsing, Richard. *You and I Have Simply Got to Stop Meeting This Way.* New York: AMACOM, 1977.

Eakins, Barbara Westbrook, and Gene Eakins. *Sex Differences in Human Communication.* Boston: Houghton Mifflin, 1978.

Fromkin, Howard, and John Sherwood. *Intergroup and Minority Relations.* La Jolla, CA: University Associates, 1976.

Hart, Lois B., and J. Gordon Schleicher. *A Conference and Workshop Planner's Manual.* New York: AMACOM, 1978.

Hon, David. "Task-Oriented Meetings with Your Superiors—How to Get In and Take Charge." *Training,* September 1978, pp. 85–88.

International Association of Business Communicators, *Without Bias: A Guidebook for Nondiscriminatory Communication,* 1977. Available from the association, 870 Market Street, Suite 928, San Francisco, CA 94102.

Johnson, David, and Frank Johnson. *Joining Together: Group Theory and Group Skills.* Available from National Humanistic Education Center, 110 Spring Street, Saratoga Springs, NY 12866.

Napier, Rodney, and Matti Gershenfeld. *Groups: Theory and Experience—Instructor's Manual.* Boston: Houghton Mifflin, 1973.

Schindler-Rainman, Eva, Ronald Lippitt, and Jack Cole. *Taking Your Meetings out of the Doldrums.* La Jolla, CA: University Associates, 1976.

Steele, Fritz, and Stephen Jenks. *The Feel of the Work Place.* Reading, MA: Addison-Wesley, 1977.

Men

Chesler, Phyllis. *About Men.* New York: Simon and Schuster, 1978.

Farrell, Warren. *The Liberated Man.* New York: Random House, 1974.

Fasteau, Marc Feigen. *The Male Machine.* New York: McGraw-Hill, 1974.

Goldberg, Herb. *The Hazards of Being Male.* New York: New American Library, 1976.

Korda, Michael. *Male Chauvinism: How It Works and How to Get Free of It.* New York: Random House, 1973.

Nichols, Jack. *Men's Liberation: A New Definition of Masculinity.* New York: Penguin Books, 1976.

Pleck, Joseph, and Jack Sawyer. *Men and Masculinity.* Englewood Cliffs, NJ: Prentice-Hall, 1975.

Snodgrass, Jon, ed. *For Men Against Sexism: A Book of Readings.* New York: Times Change Press, 1977.

5

Skills in supervision

Nancy Townsend was recently promoted to supervisor. When she revised several of the procedures for her section, she was taken aback by the objections from her subordinates.

When Sandra Attler complained about back problems, her doctor advised her to reduce her working hours. She claimed that she didn't know how to do so.

Alicia Mercurio was baffled by her subordinates' lack of interest and initiative. Although they usually completed their work on schedule, the quality was not always consistent, and employees were clearly not inspired.

Perhaps you face similar problems in your leadership position. They are not uncommon to those who have assumed responsible positions in their organizations. This chapter examines the leadership activities involved in supervision, helps you assess the skills you need, and guides you toward developing them. The goal is to provide you with supervisory skills that will help you prevent or at least handle problems similar to those described above.

What Is Supervision?

Organizations are formed and maintained because they have a specific goal—that is, to produce a product or to provide a service. In order to

meet this goal, organizations need people to make the product or
provide the service and to orchestrate the various activities involved.
These "orchestrators" are supervisors. Supervision is often thought to
be a function of the lower management levels in the organization. It is
true that most supervisory activities are performed by those at the first-
line and low levels, but leaders at all levels of the organization are, in
fact, involved.

The primary goal of supervision is the efficient accomplishment of
work. Supervisory activities involved in that process include:

Selection and orientation of new employees.
Motivation of employees.
Administration of rewards and discipline.
Arrangement for advancement.
Organization of tasks.
Monitoring of progress toward objectives.
Development of policy.

A leader must focus on both the needs of the organization (getting
the job done efficiently) and the needs of individual employees. In
addition, a leader must understand the activities performed in her work
unit as well as the way her unit functions as part of the entire
organization. A leader is thus one of the many linking pins that connect
the various parts of the organization.

How do supervisory skills differ by level? The differences are best
described as follows: Those at the lower level *direct,* those at the middle
level *review,* and those at the top level *evaluate.* With this in mind, look at
chart #15, which outlines the basic supervisory activities in an organization. First read the chart horizontally to see how each of the seven
supervisory skills are utilized at the various levels. For instance, in
monitoring progress toward objectives, the low-level leader maintains a
close watch on the work performed. She must stay in close contact with
her subordinates, immediately correct any errors, monitor progress as
the work continues, and provide a progress report to her supervisor.
The middle-level leader checks for the efficiency of procedures and the
quality of the product or service, and communicates her review to her
supervisor. The top-level leader then evaluates the report, revising the
program as needed to meet the objectives of the organization.

Next, read the chart vertically for an overview of the skills needed
by leaders at each level. This will give you the opportunity to assess the
skills needed at your current level as well as those needed to enter new
levels.

15 SUPERVISORY SKILLS

	First-line	Low	Middle	Top	Executive
Selection and orientation of new employees	• Orients new people	• Orients and trains new people	• Creates job descriptions • Selects people		
Motivation of employees	• Develops group cohesiveness • Applies motivational techniques			• Reinforces motivational climate	• Develops an effective motivational climate for the organization
Administration of rewards and discipline		• Administers rewards and punishments • Corrects undesirable behavior			
Arrangement for advancement		• Recommends people for promotion	• Develops procedures for employee training	• Determines promotion criteria and procedures	• Focuses on executive development program
Organization of tasks	• Organizes use of equipment • Assigns tasks	• Formulates efficient procedures • Matches work group activities with those of other groups	• Establishes procedures and checks	• Coordinates sub-unit objectives	
Monitoring of progress toward objectives	• Maintains personal contact with subordinates	• Differentiates hour-to-hour results	• Reviews results • Performs quality control • Checks on efficiency of operation • Communicates with levels below and above	• Evaluates goals, objectives, and programs	
Development of policy	• Enforces organizational rules				• Develops total organizational perspective

Assessing Your Supervisory Skills

Before you assess your own supervisory skills, decide if you want to focus on improving skills at your current leadership position or on developing skills for the next level above you. Then review chart #15 to determine which skills you already possess. Rate these strengths with the following code:

+3   Highly developed
+2   Somewhat developed
+1   Minimally developed

For instance, if you have had experience in writing job descriptions, but only under someone else's supervision, you might rate yourself +2.

Next, review the chart to identify those skills you'd like to develop more fully. Use a similar rating system:

−1   Needs minimal development
−2   Needs some development
−3   Needs considerable development

Suppose you need to monitor the hourly progress of those you supervise—a skill you never needed to acquire during the course of your previous work experience. You would rate yourself at −3. List the skills that need the most development on the planning sheet in chart #16, under the column marked "Skills I want to develop." Number those listed in the order in which you want to develop them. Now you can plan how to meet these needs.

This chapter focuses on the following supervisory skills:

1. *Leadership style.* What is yours? How does it affect your supervision of others? How can you learn to use a style appropriate to the situation? How do motivation techniques help to make this possible?
2. *Delegation of tasks and responsibilities.* Why is it necessary? How is it done?

On your planning sheet, check the skills you need that are covered in this chapter. Write down additional resources identified in the resources section, or those you know of from colleagues or from previous experience, that can help you with skills not covered here.

Skills I want to develop	Order of development	Found in chapter	Additional resources

Leadership Style

What is the best style for a leader? What do you do if you don't have the right style? Does it really make a difference? As you explore these questions, keep in mind that style is defined as a predictable pattern of behavior as perceived by others. Your style, in other words, is the manner in which you behave. In order to learn and use appropriate leadership styles, you must first understand your own thoughts, feelings, and attitudes about leadership.

How do you feel about leading others?

What is the relationship between the leader and the follower? What are your feelings toward each of these roles? Recall times when you have been led by others. How did you feel in your role? How did you perceive the role of the leader? Now recall the times when you functioned as a leader. How did you feel about your own role and that of your followers?

To explore your feelings about leadership further, try this experiment with another person. Place a blindfold over your eyes and have your partner take you for a 10- or 15-minute walk. Your partner should not give you any verbal directions, but should introduce you to as many new physical experiences as possible, such as walking up or down stairs, touching different textures, and moving at different speeds. After the walk, explore your feelings about being led:

1. How did you feel being led with little direction other than nonverbal communication?
2. What did you like about being the follower?
3. What didn't you like about being the follower?

Now switch roles, following the same directions. Afterward, explore your feelings about leading:

1. How did you feel about leading your partner?
2. Was it easier for you to conduct the walk (after having been a follower) than for your partner? Why or why not?
3. How did you control the movements of the follower?
4. What did you like about being the leader?
5. What didn't you like about being the leader?
6. Which of the supervisory skills listed in the chart did you use?

Next, think about your attitude toward the roles of both leader and follower. Which role did you enjoy the most? Why? These explorations help you identify what you do and do not like about each role. Such an understanding can help you function more effectively as a leader, for it is crucial that leaders *never* lose touch with what it is like to be led.

Traditional styles of leadership

There are three basic styles of leadership with which you are probably familiar: authoritarian, democratic, and laissez-faire.

Authoritarian. The authoritarian leader is completely in control, directs the activities of group members, and monitors them very closely. This leader's power emerges from the authority and status of her position in the organization. Because the authoritarian leader is in charge of the situation, she may be perceived as unwilling or uninterested in delegating power or authority to others.

Democratic. The democratic leader seeks input from subordinates, involves them in setting objectives, develops procedures, and evaluates the progress of the work. This leader's power comes from the people she leads; they participate in group discussion and decisions. The leader retains authority as long as those following grant it. A democratic leader is usually interested in delegating and sharing power and authority.

Laissez-faire. The laissez-faire leader does not interfere with the activities of subordinates; she remains in contact but does not monitor. Laissez-faire means "let people do as they please." Thus this type of leader believes in sharing power and authority.

Which of these three styles is "best"? The democratic style is frequently chosen by leaders, partly because our culture and government are based on its principles. However, none of the three styles is effective in every situation. In other words, it is sometimes more appropriate to be authoritarian than democratic, and sometimes more appropriate to let well enough alone. Adopting a style that corresponds to the situation leads to effective leadership. When a leader remains fixed in one particular style, leadership becomes ineffective.

An examination of the development of leadership within the women's movement can shed further light on leadership style. As the movement grew in size, leaders were needed to organize and implement activities. Choosing a leadership style, however, provoked intense discussions. Many women rejected any form of authoritarian leadership because it resembled the leadership style displayed by many men. In its place, the women adopted the laissez-faire model. There was no designated leader; instead, leaders were to emerge and submerge as needed. As a result, people with specialized skills were unable to initiate and utilize them fully, as any attempt to do so was taken as a threat to the desired egalitarianism. Also, people outside the group were unable to identify contacts for information or other business. A further consequence of the lack of formal structure was that it took more time to get the work done. Problems and procedures had to be reviewed by the entire group before action could be taken.

A model of leadership presently being explored by those in the women's movement is participatory democracy. In this model, all members of the group are involved in making decisions; however, unlike the leaderless group, specific leaders are chosen through a vote of the members. On the surface, this model sounds ideal—and it has worked successfully for many groups. In certain situations, however, the model does not work well. For example, in a three-member coordinating committee leading a coalition of political activists, responsibility for chairing the meetings is rotated. According to the participatory model, the three women share authority equally. However, one of the three is clearly more suited to be the leader. She is highly committed and devotes more time to the tasks to be done. She runs a meeting efficiently, and delegates work appropriately to other members. When either of the other two women chair a meeting, less gets done and group members are frustrated. All three women must participate when decisions have to be made between monthly meetings—a token of shared power that is time-consuming and often unnecessary. Thus circumstances are shaped to suit the leadership model rather than allowing the situation to determine the style of leadership needed.

An alternative: The situational leadership model

The situational leadership model focuses on the leader's ability to adapt to changing situations. This flexible approach is one of the best options for women leaders because it does not define effective leadership according to any set of personality traits, such as those masculine qualities so valued by our culture. Thus it permits women to maintain their identity within the realities of the working world.

Note that "situational" is a relatively neutral term, with little, if any, connotative meanings. Consider, by contrast, the words you associate with "authoritarian," "democratic," and "laissez-faire." Your responses probably include some of these value-laden terms:

Authoritarian	Democratic	Laissez-faire
authority	power to the people	no leader
blind obedience	majority votes	chaos
male leadership	fair and just	no structure
dictatorship		confusion
		free-for-all

"Situational leadership," on the other hand, carries no value-laden meanings; it suggests a focus on environmental variables, in which the effectiveness of a given style depends on the situation.

A situational leadership model

The concept of situational leadership originated in the 1950s, when researchers began to focus on the behaviors instead of the personality traits of leaders. These behaviors generally fell into two categories: those dealing with tasks and those dealing with relationships.

This chapter focuses on a situational leadership model developed by Paul Hersey and Kenneth Blanchard in the late 1960s and early 1970s.[1] Hersey and Blanchard organize leadership behaviors into the task and relationship categories as follows:

Task Behaviors	Relationship Behaviors
Define and organize role of followers	Determine ways to open channels of communication between leader and followers
Determine the tasks that need to be done	Delegate responsibility
Set up when, where, and how the work will be done	Provide opportunities for followers to realize their potential
Establish well-defined patterns of organization, channels of communication, and ways to accomplish work	

The situational leadership model is based on the assumption that a leader does not operate in isolation, but is influenced by a number of interdependent variables. These variables include (1) the goals, objectives, and norms of the organization; (2) the demands inherent in the leader's job and her level in the organization; and (3) the expectations of those to whom the leader is accountable (her bosses), those for whom she is responsible (her followers), and those with whom she is equal (her colleagues).

The situational leadership model defines effective leadership as the ability to identify the variables in any given situation or environment (the organization's expectation, job demands, and expectations of others) and to adapt the leadership style that most closely matches the situation.

Figure 5 graphically shows this model. Note that the task behavior dimension is along the bottom of the graph and the relationship behavior is along the left-hand side. Follow the line from the lower right-hand corner toward the left, which traces the direction a leader

Figure 5. The situational leadership model.

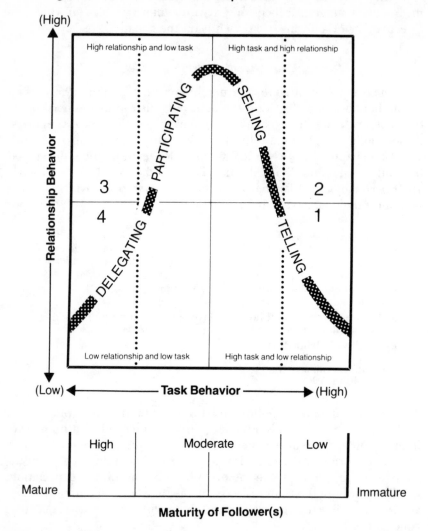

needs to move her followers. Thus her goal is to begin at the point the group members are and gradually adapt her style as the group's needs change.

For example, the leadership style found in the "Telling" block requires more of the task behaviors (described above) and more structuring of the group's activities so that the tasks will get done. As the group increases its ability and experience, then the leadership style would move into "Selling," with a balance of task and relationship leadership behaviors. The third stage of a leader's style is called "Participating," and it is here that the relationships dimension is emphasized. When a leader moves into the fourth stage ("Delegating") it appears that she has worked herself out of a job. She leaves the employees alone to handle their jobs and to meet their own social and emotional needs. Actually, the leader is never out of work, but can use this opportunity to move on to new challenges for herself. She may pursue new tasks or begin supervising new people who are at earlier stages in the cycle of leadership styles.

The leader's starting point on the cycle for any given task is *always* determined by her followers' abilities, knowledge, and attitudes. Hersey and Blanchard grouped these variables into two "maturity" dimensions, as shown below.

Job Maturity Dimension	*Psychological Maturity Dimension*
Past job experience	Willingness to take responsibility
Job knowledge	Achievement motivation
Understanding of job requirements	Commitment
Problem-solving ability	Persistence
Ability to meet job deadlines	Work attitude
Follow-through ability	Initiative
Ability to take responsibility	Independence

Your job as a leader is to assess the maturity (or readiness) of your followers for each of the tasks in which they are involved so you can make a more informed decision in your choice of leadership style. The "Maturity Scale—Manager Rating Form" developed by Hersey and Blanchard can help you determine the readiness of those you lead. The "Maturity Scale—Self-Rating Form" can help assess your own readiness for a particular task. (See the resources section for information on obtaining these and other situational leadership tools described below.)

Once you know the readiness of your followers, you can determine an appropriate leadership style. As the maturity grid at the bottom of Figure 5 indicates, if you assess your followers to be low in "maturity," the most appropriate style would be in quadrants 1 and 2. Moderate "maturity" would require a style in quadrants 2 and 3, and high "maturity" would require a style in quadrants 3 and 4. Theoretically, if you have assessed the readiness and needs of your followers correctly and have matched your style to the situation, your leadership will be effective.

Hersey and Blanchard also developed a two-part form called the Leadership Effectiveness and Adaptability Description (LEAD) to help leaders assess their style. The "LEAD—Self" questionnaire describes twelve incidents and asks you to indicate how you would respond. The scores indicate both your "dominant" and "subordinate" leadership styles as well as how flexible you are in adapting your style to changing situations. The "LEAD—Other" questionnaire is designed for others (subordinates, superiors, and associates) to provide feedback on your leadership style. Their perceptions can be compared with yours.

Applying situational leadership

Theories are only guides. It is up to you to take the concept of situational leadership and apply it to your own work situation. To increase your understanding of the situational leadership theory, become an astute observer of other people's leadership styles. Look for as many opportunities as possible to observe others as they lead. For instance, analyze the styles of your boss and her or his boss. Observe the style of the leader in any professional or community meeting that you attend. Observe the style of anyone in a leadership position in movies or television programs. Read biographies of famous leaders, male and female.

Use chart **#17** to record your observations of other leaders. The task and relationship behaviors used by Hersey and Blanchard to describe major leadership activities are listed on the left side of the chart. Make notes on different people you observe. Next, review the pattern of behaviors you have observed and decide which quadrant the person's style falls into. Was the task accomplished? What was the morale of the group? If the task was achieved and morale was high, the leader was effective.

Before you apply the theory to those you lead, it is important that you teach them the basic concepts so that you and they can have a common framework and vocabulary for discussing the various aspects of the job. You should also obtain and complete the "LEAD—Self" questionnaire and the "Maturity Scale—Self-Rating Form."

In addition, you may want your followers to complete the "LEAD—Other" questionnaire (either anonymously or openly) so that you can compare your perceptions of your style with those of your employees. Discuss the results with the group. Be open to your followers' observations and suggestions and ask for explanations if their comments are too general. The guidelines for giving effective feedback in Chapter 3 may be useful here.

The next step in implementing the theory is to "contract" with your followers — that is, to have each one determine which leadership style best suits her or his needs. The "Maturity Scale—Manager Rating Form" can help employees (and you) identify their readiness for each major work assignment.

Hold a conference with each employee and compare your assessments. Discuss what each person needs from you to carry out her or his

A. Task behaviors
1. Organized and defined roles of group members

2. Explained what to do, and when, where, and how to do it

3. Established well-defined patterns of organization and channels of communication

B. Relationship behaviors
1. Opened channels of communication

2. Delegated responsibility

3. Gave followers opportunity to develop their potential

4. Gave socioemotional support; extended friendship; built trust

C. Analysis
1. Which style predominated?

2. Was the task accomplished?

3. What was the morale of the group?

work assignments. Be specific. For example, if someone tells you that she wants you to operate in quadrant 2 (high task, low relationship), find out what her request actually means. Does she want to meet with you daily or weekly to review her work? Does she want another employee to give her directions on tasks and to monitor her progress? In other words, when a person asks for a specific "style" from you, translate the request into procedures that are realistic and workable.

Put your agreement in writing so that both you and your followers are clear about what you expect from each other. Because the goal is to move each person through the "life cycle" as she or he is ready, it is important to review progress periodically, to assess changes in task and psychological maturity, and to revise the contract when necessary. Ask your followers continually how they perceive their own progress and readiness for more responsibility. Observe them and compare your observations. Provide opportunities for growth when an employee is ready.

These activities entail a considerable time commitment on your part. But assessing your followers' needs and determining the best leadership style for them will pay dividends in the successful achievement of tasks and high morale—the hallmarks of effective leadership.

Expanding your leadership style

Effective supervision requires that the leader adapt her style to meet the situation. Since situations change continually, leaders need to build a repertoire of different styles. Expanding your repertoire of leadership styles may require a major commitment of time. Are you willing to make that commitment?

The crucial first step is to recognize that change is needed. If you are at this point, you've come a long way. Next, commit yourself to personal growth by attending special workshops or seeking counseling. Focus on one aspect of your personality at a time and give yourself a specific objective. For instance, you may decide that you need to reduce your tendency to control others so that you are better able to delegate authority. Focusing on one aspect of change at a time and defining a specific objective will increase your chances of success.

Many people find certain leadership styles to be incompatible with their personal philosophy. For instance, the high task, low relationship style is frequently rejected by women as too inhumane or too reminiscent of masculine styles. As previously mentioned, some feminists have rejected traditional hierarchical styles and are experimenting with other systems. It is important to be clear about your philosophy—that is, how you prefer to work with other people—and to understand what methods are compatible with your beliefs and values.

Do any of your values or beliefs place restrictions on your range of leadership styles? If so, it is important that you be aware of how these limitations can affect your role as leader. You may find it necessary to avoid assuming certain leadership responsibilities if they call for a style that conflicts with your values. It is advantageous to you, your followers, and your organization to recognize and be explicit about your limitations.

Delegation

Delegation is another skill basic to effective supervision. The goal of delegation is to assign responsibility to others so that:

1. Tasks are accomplished.
2. Followers have an opportunity to assume responsibility and to increase their initiative and independence.
3. Work is continued even in your absence.

How do you rate as a delegator? Assess your own delegation skills by filling in chart #18. Read each of the statements and determine if you seldom, sometimes, or frequently behave in the manner described. Fill in only one column per statement. Score yourself as follows on the odd-numbered items:

5	Seldom
3	Sometimes
1	Frequently

Score the even-numbered items this way:

1	Seldom
3	Sometimes
5	Frequently

Add up your totals. How do you rate? If you scored between 40 and 50, you are generally an effective delegator. If you scored between 30 and 39, you are a minimally effective delegator. If you scored under 30, you need in-depth study of delegation skills.

Delegation calls for planning ahead, coordinating activities, establishing goals, defining authority and responsibility, giving tasks to subordinates, and trusting their ability to carry them out. Look back at the chart. Which of these activities are your strengths? Your weaknesses?

---

18   DELEGATING SKILLS ASSESSMENT

Statement	Seldom	Some-times	Fre-quently
1. I find it easier and quicker to do most tasks myself as opposed to delegating them to others.	_____	_____	_____
2. At the beginning of each workday or week, I have a plan of action that outlines tasks for my employees to complete.	_____	_____	_____
3. When I want something done right, I do it myself.	_____	_____	_____
4. I know the skills, talents, experience, and job knowledge of my employees so that I am ready to match their "job maturity" to particular tasks.	_____	_____	_____
5. I find myself tied down by the details of my job so that I lack time to supervise employees, work on new projects, keep up with my reading, or develop delegation plans.	_____	_____	_____
6. When a person doesn't fulfill his or her responsibility, we determine the cause of the problem and work out a solution.	_____	_____	_____
7. After I delegate a task, I suggest methods that have worked for me in the past.	_____	_____	_____
8. The employee who does a task especially well is not left with that job exclusively. I assign her new tasks to try.	_____	_____	_____
9. Once I delegate, I leave the employee alone until she decides to report back to me.	_____	_____	_____
10. I try to create a work climate that is conducive to delegation.	_____	_____	_____
Total score			

Women and delegation

The skill of delegation is of particular importance to women. Hennig and Jardim have found that women moving up in an organization have difficulty delegating responsibility to those they lead. They describe a hypothetical situation in which a woman progresses in her career over a ten-year period. After an initial investment of time, she rises to a supervisory role that suits her beautifully. She is "responsible for all her old assignments, the supervision of subordinates, and the added work, and involved in ensuring that nothing leaves her small department unless it is perfect. To ensure this she often prefers to do the job herself. Her supervisory style is a close one; she is a scrupulous checker, a dotter of *i*'s and a crosser of *t*'s. . . . It is not a style which breeds initiative, nor does it lend itself to delegating responsibility."[2]

Hennig and Jardim found that this set style led others to rate her as an "outstanding supervisor" but bypassed her as possessing qualities for management. These supervisors lacked the long-term dimension needed to advance her career.

This rigid style may work at the supervisory level, but at higher levels a style of close supervision, nondelegation, and self-reliance is inappropriate. The woman who continues to behave as a supervisor when she is an executive will have difficulty. She clearly needs to learn how to delegate.

How do you feel about delegation? Think of a time when you as a leader needed to delegate tasks to others, but didn't. Why was it hard to assign the work to others? What happened as a result? How did you feel and how did the others act and feel? Think of a time when you as a leader did delegate tasks to others. What happened? How did the others act and feel?

What kinds of tasks are easier for you to delegate? What kinds are more difficult? How do you react when subordinates don't follow through on their assignments? What do you gain or lose when you delegate tasks?

Recall a time when a supervisor delegated work to you. How did you act and what did you feel? Recall a time when you knew that you could handle a particular task but your leader did not trust you to do so without close guidance. How did you react and what did you feel? Finally, recall a time when a change in roles demanded a change in your style of delegating. How much difficulty did you have in making that shift?

Your answers to these questions will help you focus on those aspects of delegation you need to work on most. Keep your answers in mind as you read the following section.

Steps in delegation

Seven steps are involved in delegating work to others.

1. Develop a climate for delegation.
2. Determine your objectives.
3. Know your workers.
4. Develop a plan.
5. Communicate your expectations.
6. Monitor progress.
7. Evaluate results and assign new work.

Figure 6. The delegation cycle.

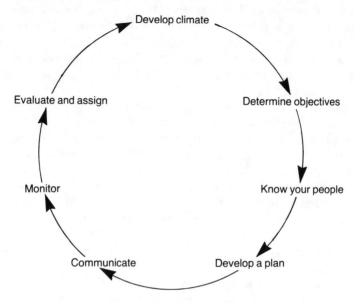

Develop climate

Evaluate and assign

Determine objectives

Monitor

Know your people

Communicate

Develop a plan

These seven steps are cyclical, as Figure 6 shows. Each time a task is completed, you start the cycle again, building on previous experiences, extending your followers' knowledge and skills, and adjusting your leadership style accordingly.

1. *Develop a climate.* What type of climate is conducive to delegation? Recall those times when others delegated tasks to you and the work was accomplished. Most likely, both you and your boss felt good about the outcome. What were some of the variables in that healthy climate? One factor was undoubtedly an atmosphere of trust. Mutual trust must exist between leader and follower—trust that each will be honest about the objectives of the task, her ability and interest in performing the task, and progress toward its achievement.

A second factor is a willingness to learn. The leader and the follower need to admit that they don't know all the answers and that something can be learned from every mistake and success. Such an attitude encourages growth. A challenging task can be attempted without fear of failure, since the knowledge gained from the attempt is viewed as valuable. Once a task has been achieved or a job has been thoroughly learned, additional challenges can be taken on. In this climate the leader and follower are encouraged to ask, "What else am I ready to learn and try?"

A third factor is open, clear, and continual communication. The communication skills of attentive listening, paraphrasing, and giving and receiving feedback, as presented in Chapter 3, are beneficial in opening channels so that both the leader and the follower have the opportunity to clarify the assigned task, obtain information on procedures, and monitor progress.

2. *Determine your objectives.* As a leader, you have an overview of what needs to be done and thus can determine the most important objectives. (The guidelines for writing objectives in Chapter 9 may be useful here.)

3. *Know your workers.* As noted earlier in the section on situational leadership, you cannot determine the most appropriate leadership style without knowing the readiness of your followers. Hersey and Blanchard's "Maturity Scale" is especially useful here because it helps you pinpoint who is ready to do what tasks and thus to determine the degree of authority they can successfully handle.

4. *Develop a plan.* Once you have identified your objectives and assessed your personnel, you are ready to develop a plan—to determine the tasks to be accomplished and an overall timetable for their achievements.

5. *Communicate your expectations.* Your next task is to communicate the plan to your followers. Hold a joint conference to review the resources needed to accomplish the task, discuss any barriers to accomplishing the task, determine a schedule of assignments, and outline the boundaries of authority. A word of caution about the conference: Do not supply too much information at this time. In a climate of trust and open communication, your followers will tell you how much they need to know. Use paraphrasing to be sure your messages have been received accurately.

6. *Monitor progress.* At this point, the plan outlined and agreed upon in earlier steps is put into action. Because you are ultimately responsible for task achievement, it is important that you be aware of the progress being made toward work objectives. Develop a method of checking on schedules, quality of work, and assignments of responsibility and discuss it with your followers. You and your followers may determine that daily or even hourly checks are essential. Decide whether you will conduct your reviews through verbal discussion, written memos, or informal observation.

7. *Evaluate results and assign new work.* The final step is to evaluate results. Was the task accomplished as agreed? Was the outcome satisfactory? Was it completed on time? What did each employee learn? Did her job and psychological maturity increase? What could you have done to help her be more successful?

Remember that your goal as a leader is not only to accomplish tasks but also to increase your employees' knowledge and skills. Discuss positive and negative experiences openly with your followers. Reinforce

positive learning experiences so they can be carried into new assignments. After reviewing the results, you and your employee are ready to
plan for future tasks.

With an understanding of the steps involved in delegation and an
awareness of potential pitfalls, you are ready to apply these ideas to
your own work situation. Think of a circumstance that would necessitate delegation and go through each of the steps outlined. Afterward,
answer again the questions found at the beginning of the section on
delegation and see if your delegating skills have improved.

Record the key words of the steps for delegation on an index card
for easy reference at your desk. On the back, write your personal goals
for improving your style of delegating. Refer to the cards often to
review the skills in the context of *your* personal goals. Remember that
orchestrating the work of those whom you lead is a challenge. An
understanding and application of the concept of situational leadership
and the techniques of delegation can help you lead your followers
toward the successful accomplishment of tasks plus high job satisfaction.

REFERENCES

1. Paul Hersey and Kenneth H. Blanchard, *Management of Organizational
   Behavior,* 2nd ed. (Englewood Cliffs, NJ: Prentice-Hall, 1972).
2. Margaret Hennig and Anne Jardim, *The Managerial Woman* (New York:
   Doubleday, 1977), p. 39.

RESOURCES

Anthologies

Gurko, Miriam. *The Ladies of Seneca Falls.* New York: Macmillan, 1974. Accounts
   of the lives of significant suffragists and leaders, including Lucretia Mott,
   Lucy Stone, Susan B. Anthony, and Elizabeth Cady Stanton.

Merriam, Eve, ed., *Growing Up Female in America: Ten Lives.* Ten different
   women, living in different times and places and from different social and
   economic backgrounds, describe their lives in their own words.

Nathan, Dorothy. *Women of Courage.* New York: Random House, 1964. Profiles
   of five American women: Susan B. Anthony, Jane Addams, Mary McLeod
   Bethune, Amelia Earhart, and Margaret Mead.

Biographies and Autobiographies

Susan B. Anthony. This woman suffrage leader worked closely with Elizabeth
   Cady Stanton to win the vote for American women. Biographies include
   The Life and Work of Susan B. Anthony, 3 vols., by Ida Harper (1898–1908)
   (reproduction edition, New York: Arno Press, 1969), and *Susan B. Anthony:
   Rebel, Crusader, and Humanitarian,* by Alma Lutz (1959) (reproduction
   edition, New York: Zenger Publishers, 1976).

Shirley Chisholm. Her autobiography, *Unbought and Unbossed*, tells how our first congresswoman challenged some of America's most cherished and carefully guarded prejudices. See also Susan Brownmiller, *Shirley Chisholm* (New York: Anchor Books, 1972).

Emma Goldman. Goldman was an alien, a practicing anarchist, a labor agitator, a pacifist, a feminist, a proponent of free love and birth control, a Communist, and a street fighter for justice. Her autobiography is called *Living My Life*, 2 vols. (New York: Da Capo Press, 1931).

Sarah and Angelina Grimka. These two rebel Southern women became voluntary exiles in order to live according to conscience and speak out for the abolition of slavery. Their story is told by Gerda Lerner in *The Grimka Sisters from South Carolina* (New York: Schocken Books, 1973).

Golda Meir. Her autobiography, *My Life* (New York: Putnam's Sons, 1975), traces her early life in the United States, her immigration to Israel, and her political career there.

Margaret Sanger. Her book, *Margaret Sanger: An Autobiography* (New York: Dover, 1938), traces her battle to establish birth control as a basic human right. See also her biography by Lawrence Lader and Milton Meltzer, *Margaret Sanger, Pioneer of Birth Control* (New York: Dell, 1947).

Margaret Chase Smith. The first woman to be a U.S. Senator is described in Alice Fleming, *The Senator from Maine* (New York: Dell, 1976).

Elizabeth Cady Stanton. Her autobiography is called *Eighty Years and More: Reminiscence 1815–1877* (New York: Schocken Books, 1971). Biographies include *Created Equal: A Biography of Elizabeth Cady Stanton* by Alma Lutz (New York: Octagon Books, 1973).

Ida B. Wells. A crusader against black oppression from post-Reconstruction to 1931, Wells tells her story in *Crusade for Justice* (University of Chicago Press, 1972).

General

Hennig, Margaret, and Anne Jardim. *The Managerial Woman*. New York: Doubleday, 1977.

Hersey, Paul, and Kenneth Blanchard. *Management of Organizational Behavior*, 3rd ed. Englewood Cliffs, NJ: Prentice-Hall, 1977.

Hilgert, Raymond, and Theo Haimann. *Supervision: Concepts and Practices of Management*. Chicago: South-Western, 1977.

Maslow Abraham. *Motivation and Personality*. New York: Harper & Row, 1970.

The situational leadership tools described in this chapter can be ordered from Learning Resources Corporation, 7594 Eads Avenue, La Jolla, CA 92037. Ask for "LEAD—Self," "LEAD—Other," "Maturity Scale—Self-Rating Form," and "Maturity Scale—Manager Rating Form."

6

The leader as counselor

COUNSELING is an integral part of leadership. Think of the times when your followers had personal problems that affected their work, or needed guidance on career development or work performance. Counseling activities can be divided into three types: performance counseling, personal counseling, and career counseling. All three activities require a climate conducive to growth, an ability to listen and guide others, and objectivity. Thus counseling interacts with the leadership skills of communication, human relations, and supervision. More specifically, counseling requires attentive listening, giving positive and negative feedback, and adapting your leadership styles to the situation.

Counseling in the Organization

How do the leader's skills in counseling differ from level to level? As chart #19 shows, those in first-line and low-level supervisory positions spend more time on performance counseling than on personal counseling. Daily contact with employees requires the ability to monitor, discuss, and correct behaviors. Leaders at this level must be in tune with signs of personal problems that may interfere with job performance. Their responsibility is to refer troubled employees to appropriate individuals in the organization (higher-level managers, medical staff) or to outside agencies.

The middle-level leader focuses on both personal and performance counseling. Because the leader at this level considers the needs of the total organization—its direction, purpose, and demands—she has already adapted to the behavioral demands inherent in her position and

19 COUNSELING SKILLS

	First-line/Low	Middle	Top/Executive
Performance counseling	• Develops a climate conducive to constructive performance • Emphasizes job criteria • Clarifies job expectations • Reviews positive and negative behaviors that affect work performance • Helps employers develop and implement plans to correct unacceptable behaviors • Communicates individual and group performance to boss	• Gains knowledge of performance appraisal systems, goal setting, management by objectives • Develops system to be used • Teaches system to subordinates • Reviews performance of subordinates	• Establishes policy for effective performance evaluation • Directs and monitors establishment of performance evaluative systems
Personal counseling	• Applies listening and interviewing skills to identify problems • Refers employees to appropriate organizational personnel or community agency	• Develops counseling skills to identify personal problems of employees • Counsels employees • Refers serious problems to other agencies • Establishes special counseling programs (for example, drug addiction) • Recommends employees for dismissal	• Establishes policy for role and practice of personal counseling • Conducts some one-to-one counseling with managers • Identifies people whose personal problems might affect them professionally • Identifies appropriate referral agencies and programs • Endorses need and resources for special programs
Career counseling	• Cooperatively assesses and recommends employees for appropriate career development opportunities	• Gains knowledge of career development techniques and assessment tools • Conducts periodic assessments of employees' potential and needs • Trains subordinates on how to identify employees' potential	• Establishes policy for including career counseling as leadership activity • Allocates resources for implementing career counseling

understands the consequences of inappropriate conduct on work performance and organizational reputation. Therefore, she is in an excellent position to help employees explore their strengths, needs, and aspirations as they would fit into the goals and norms of the organization.

The middle-level leader is responsible for identifying subordinates with the potential to rise within the organization and for establishing procedures for their advancement. Women leaders at the middle level have the opportunity to facilitate the upward mobility of other women by using the formal selection process and/or by becoming mentors. (Mentorship is discussed in Chapter 10.)

Leaders at the top levels do not engage in extensive counseling. Their responsibility is to set a climate that facilitates counseling by others in the organization. With recommendations from middle managers, they set policy, endorse practices, and allocate resources for performance evaluation systems and for personal or career counseling programs. For example, an executive might endorse a company policy that gives employees several opportunities to resolve personal problems instead of demanding their immediate dismissal. The top manager may set up counseling procedures for identifying personal problems early or may arrange for supervisors to receive special training in this skill. In addition, the executive may prepare and circulate a comprehensive list of community agencies for company personnel.

Assessing Your Counseling Skills

You are now ready to assess your counseling skills. Again, decide whether you want to focus on improving skills at your current level or on developing skills for the level above you. Review chart **#19** to determine which skills you already possess. Rate these strengths with the following code:

+3	Highly developed
+2	Somewhat developed
+1	Minimally developed

For example, you might have had plenty of experience explaining the expectations of jobs and can do it comfortably and efficiently. Thus, you rate yourself +3. Next, review the chart to identify those skills you would like to develop more fully. Use a similar rating system:

−1	Needs minimal development
−2	Needs some development
−3	Needs considerable development

For instance, if you have never established a special counseling program (such as assistance to alcoholics) you might rate yourself − 2 or − 3.

List the skills that need the most development on the planning sheet in chart **#20,** the column marked "Skills I want to develop." Number those listed in the order in which you want to develop them.

This chapter focuses on personal counseling, presenting a philosophy and techniques for helping employees, and on performance evaluation, with a review of options for assessing the work of others. The chapter does not include career counseling. Parts of Chapters 1, 9, and 10 provide a model for making a career decision. In addition, many resources on career counseling are listed at the end of this chapter.

Counseling for Personal Problems

It is important to recognize that personal problems of all kinds are carried into the workplace; to ignore this fact is to put your head in the sand. You may have heard the maxim that work and personal problems should be kept totally separate. This view is unrealistic. What happens to people in their private lives inevitably affects their performance at work.

Personal problems may relate to starting and ending relationships, raising children, using drugs, poor health, loneliness, conflicts with other people, and money. There is no doubt that everyone has problems. The frequency and severity of such problems may vary, but the problems themselves are a normal part of living. Leaders in an organization, therefore, must arrange to help employees find solutions to personal problems in order to preserve their ability to work effectively.

If you are a low- or middle-level leader, you must learn to recognize the signs of problems, use appropriate counseling techniques, and refer severe problems to other individuals in the organization or to agencies in the community. How do you determine if a problem is "normal" or "severe"? If an employee occasionally comes to work on Monday morning with a hangover or in low spirits, chances are the problem is not severe. The key word, however, is "occasionally." If the employee regularly shows signs of heavy drinking or depression, it is likely that she or he has a serious problem. People with severe, long-term problems should be referred to either a special program in the organization (some now have programs for drug abuse) or an outside agency. If you are at the middle or top level of the organization, you are responsible for identifying the resources available for helping with

20   PLANNING SHEET FOR SKILLS IN COUNSELING

Skills I want to develop	Order of development	Found in chapter	Additional resources

these problems. If you are an executive, it is your responsibility to set policies that allocate resources to support those with problems.

A Philosophy of Helping Others

The philosophy of counseling developed by Harvey Jackins assumes that each individual knows what is best for her.[1] Because present wants and needs are influenced by past experiences, each person must work to separate the feelings surrounding past hurts from the new situation so that she can more clearly determine the best direction to take. With this philosophy, the leader as a counselor *facilitates* the person's search. The leader serves as a guide rather than an adviser. As such, she does not have to know "the answers." As the proverb says, "If you give a person a fish, she will eat tonight; if you teach her how to fish, she will eat forever." Giving— or trying to give—answers is a short-term solution. Providing a means to find answers is a long-term solution. It is important to understand that the leader's role is to facilitate, not to direct or solve.

Creating a "Safe" Environment

If such a philosophy is compatible with your beliefs and values, your next step is to create an environment to put it into practice. In other words, you must make the atmosphere "safe" enough to facilitate others' growth. What factors create such an atmosphere? Here are a few to consider:

1. Others around you are willing to be open and grow. They do not convey a "this is good for you, but I don't need it" attitude. As the leader, you must model the behavior and attitudes you expect from others. In other words, practice what you preach. Behavior speaks louder than words.

2. There is no judgment. Others involved do not make value statements or evaluate how you feel or what you do. A leader avoids evaluative statements and insists that others do the same.

3. There is a mutual trust that all conversations are confidential. The person with the problem needs to know that the information she reveals will not be used against her.

4. The person with the problem chooses what she wants to disclose and when. If the employee feels pressured to talk or forced to talk at a time and a place not of her choosing, she may become anxious and insecure. The employee must determine the when, the where, and the what.

5. The leader-counselor talks less and listens more. The employee should do most of the talking—not just 50 percent but at least 75 percent of the time. The leader-counselor listens carefully for thoughts and feelings, paraphrases what she hears, and asks questions to help the

employee clarify her attitudes. The leader-counselor avoids giving either instruction or advice.

6. The leader-counselor is open to values and attitudes different from her own. She conveys her acceptance verbally and nonverbally. She is willing to experiment with new values and attitudes and encourages others to do the same.

An environment safe for growth exists when the leader-counselor communicates a desire to understand the other person and to help the employee help herself. Such an environment takes time to develop. Many people have felt safe so seldom in their lives that they mistrust any attempt to encourage them to risk again. Nonetheless, any effort to help people is worthwhile. Start with yourself. Model the philosophy. Seek out private places for confidential sharing. Learn and use counseling techniques. Be open to signs of others' readiness to share.

Staying Alert to Problems

How do you know if a problem exists? Be alert to signs of problems: What is the person saying and not saying? Is the employee increasingly pessimistic or depressed? Has she withdrawn from usual conversation? How does the employee speak? Does her voice quiver? Does she speak more softly than usual?

How does the person look? Are there signs of fatigue, slumped shoulders, sluggishness, weight gain or loss, dull eyes, poor skin tone? Has the person's work performance fallen below standard? Is there an increase in absenteeism? Is the employee engaging in an unusual frenzy of activity?

A person who regularly shows signs of fatigue, withdrawal, depression, and inability to perform work assignments is likely to have a serious problem. As a leader, your responsibility is to watch for clues, provide the employee with help, and try to prevent such behaviors from becoming routine.

A second way to determine if problems exist is to check routinely on what's happening in people's lives. *Sincerely* ask, "How are things with you?" Then listen attentively for clues about potential or existing problems. A successful woman stockbroker uses this method with her clients, always inquiring about their personal lives. Rather than dismiss the personal information she receives with a short comment, she pursues the "opening in the door." She sets up a time to talk to them later that night and returns to the business at hand. She then calls from her home. This woman has proved that a successful businessperson can become involved in others' personal lives without compromising her work objectives. In fact, her total sales are consistently at the top in the industry.

The leader-counselor needs to check with employees regularly about their lives through both informal and formal means. Clues gleaned over a cup of coffee can be pursued later in a more private place. Some leaders have lunch with a different employee every day to become more familiar with the goals, activities, and problems of their people.

An understanding of the stages of adult development can improve your counseling abilities. Gail Sheehy's *Passages* describes some of the predictable stages through which most adults pass.[2] Although such information should not be generalized to all people, it does provide guidelines to what many men and women face at different points in their lives. The problems faced by a 27-year-old, a 35-year-old, and a 57-year-old are different.

Counseling techniques

Women learn valuable counseling skills as part of "growing up female." For example, most women have learned to listen well, for both content and feelings. Women have learned to "read" the feelings of others, even if they say nothing. Many women can tell if something is wrong as soon as a person walks into the room. This skill, sometimes called female intuition, is valuable to leaders. The ability to look for feelings and to empathize with others is essential for effective counseling.

Research shows that the most effective counselors are aware of their body language as they interact with others. Use your eyes, body, and ears when you counsel.

Eyes. Look at the employee. Keep a steady eye contact that says, "I'm listening."

Body. Position your body so you can easily see and hear the other person. Lean toward her. Never turn your shoulder or place a big desk or table between you. Sit fairly close.

Ears. Listen, listen, and listen. Ask questions that encourage the employee to expand on the problem. Paraphrase what she says to make sure you heard correctly. Do not interrupt in the middle of the "story" or interject your own ideas.

Another way to facilitate other people's growth is to apply the problem-solving techniques found in Chapter 8. Be sure that the person being counseled agrees to and is familiar with this process. You can then lead the employee through the steps of identifying the problem, analyzing the causes, searching for solutions, and developing a plan of action.

Counseling others about their personal problems can facilitate the accomplishment of work assignments. By doing so, you will be meeting both organizational goals and individual goals, which can be compatible with each other.

Performance Counseling

What are your experiences with your own performance reviews? For example, did your supervisor spend most of the time telling you what to do or asking you what you thought about the task and your performance? Did your supervisor encourage you and accept your ideas and feelings? Did the supervisor use any of your ideas? Was your work formally reviewed once a week, once a month, every six months, or once a year?

In recalling your experiences, you may discover that your work reviews, like many others, were not productive, were too infrequent, and were not looked forward to in a positive way. Although you probably cannot control how others review your work, you as a leader can improve the quality of the conferences you hold with your employees on the progress of their work.

Leaders frequently receive inadequate training in the skill of monitoring others' work. As a result, employees lose out on an important learning experience—one that can facilitate their professional and personal growth. As a leader, your function is to create an environment and to develop appropriate tools for increasing the skills and knowledge of your employees. This, in turn, ensures better work performance. Communicate your desire to understand your employees and to help them sharpen their problem-solving abilities. Your goal is to move employees from dependence to independence so they become more self-reliant and productive.

Counseling on work performance should be neither evaluative nor negative. Evaluation breeds defensiveness, a state in which growth is unlikely. When threat is minimized, the opportunity to share useful information is maximized. The performance counseling session is a time not only for giving praise but for reinforcing appropriate behaviors and attitudes and for setting new goals. It is a two-way communication process in which information, resources, feelings, and ideas are exchanged. Performance counseling recognizes the relationship between employees' values, attitudes, and lifestyle and their work performance. It balances praise with constructive criticism and emphasizes sharing and goal setting for the purpose of enhancing personal and professional growth.

Performance counseling systems

This section describes four different performance counseling systems: normative, mastery, written narrative, and self-evaluative. Each of these approaches has certain advantages and can be used effectively in combination with one or more of the others. Learn how to use them all to increase your flexibility as a leader and to ensure that the needs of individual employees will be met.

How do you decide when an approach is appropriate? Ask yourself the following questions:

—Will this approach stimulate the employee's growth?
—Does it include clearly written, specific, and measurable objectives?
—Does the approach consider the employee's strengths and weaknesses and provide a way of determining possible directions for improvement?
—Is there sufficient time to utilize it properly?
—What preparations (training, development of tools, testing of materials) are needed?

Now study the systems described below and determine which one (or combination) best meets your needs, the employee's needs, and the organization's needs.

THE NORMATIVE SYSTEM

The normative system evaluates a person's performance in relation to set standards or norms. These norms may vary from organization to organization. For instance, one organization's norm for appropriate dress may be based on what most people wear in that organization alone; another firm's norm may be based on what is worn throughout the entire industry.

The normative system uses scales for assessment. The scale may range from "excellent" to "unsatisfactory," "good" to "bad," or "appropriate" to "inappropriate." Or the scale may use percentages to record how frequently a work objective is met. For example: "Arrives to work promptly 50 percent of the time." Letter and numerical systems similar to school grades (A-B-C-D-F, or 90-80-70-65) may also be used.

A number of researchers favor the normative system, arguing that it has many advantages. First, they point out that information about the employee's work performance can be obtained quickly and efficiently. The reviewer can readily read numbers or key words. The information is concise. Second, these researchers maintain that the method can be used as a predictor of future success. For instance, a person's high score on an aptitude test given as part of the selection process for a supervisor of bank tellers may be taken as an indication that this person would perform effectively as a manager of a branch office. Third, they believe that the normative system, in comparing one employee against another, reflects the reality that competition is part of life. Fourth, they argue that a normative system motivates employees to work harder and inspires them toward greater achievement.

However, contrary research and evidence also exist. First, although the normative system may be efficient, it does not always provide sufficient information to help an employee learn and grow. The data provided may be *too* concise. Second, the evaluative nature of the system may breed defensiveness in employees. Once defensiveness develops, motivation may drop. Third, while many aspects of life are competitive, there is increasing evidence of the need for cooperation to solve complex problems. Fourth, success at one level does not automatically ensure success at another level or in a different position, so using results of performance tests to predict a person's future success may be unreliable.

Another problem is that most norms are not tested for validity. For instance, inability to lift certain weights has been accepted as a norm for women. A test of validity for this norm would reveal that some women can lift heavy objects—and that some men cannot. The untested and unproven norm, however, has been used to determine which jobs can and cannot be filled by women and has thus limited their career options.

The Mastery System

The mastery system charts an employee's step-by-step progress in mastering certain tasks. The employee completes the easiest tasks before moving to the next, proceeding at her or his own pace. The method does not involve comparisons of performance to a standard or to peers. Instead, measurement tools are used to identify individual needs and to provide feedback for future growth. With the mastery system, there is always time to learn, perform, and accomplish more.

Two methods are used to record accomplishments: completion acknowledgment and criterion reference. In the former, completed tasks (and their dates) are recorded by the leader, often on a checklist. The checklist enables the leader and the employee to see at a glance what must still be done.

In criterion reference method, a level of proficiency is established for each task to be mastered. The task may involve acquiring a skill, completing a project or activity, or learning a concept. The criterion reference system provides more specific information than completion acknowledgment; it indicates how well each task was done. It thus allows the employee and the supervisor to plan jointly for future activities and to evaluate progress toward stated goals.

There are many advantages to the mastery system. Work performance is assessed within a context of individual growth. The system encourages exploration, creativity, and individualized leadership. Competitive pressure is removed and an atmosphere of cooperation is created. The leader becomes a helper, not an evaluator. Finally, the employee participates more fully in the planning process.

The mastery system does, however, have its drawbacks. For example, a simple checklist of tasks completed does not provide sufficient feedback to determine the causes of uncompleted work or ways to improve. In addition, considerable time is needed to provide individualized instruction, develop tools to measure progress, train leaders and employees, and complete and share the recorded information. Finally, if employees are accustomed to an evaluative approach based on competition, the introduction of the mastery system may be met with some mistrust. With time and patience, you can help them adjust to the new technique.

THE WRITTEN NARRATIVE SYSTEM

In the written narrative system, a report is prepared on each employee's performance. The report describes progress in the accomplishment of tasks or the attainment of skills, and the appropriateness of certain attitudes and behaviors. The assessment may be based on set criteria, a checklist, and/or the leader's observations.

This system provides detailed information on the employee's progress. It can communicate the total picture focusing on the procedures used to accomplish certain tasks and on the particular needs of the employee. The chief disadvantage of the system is that it demands a great deal of time for preparation.

THE SELF-EVALUATIVE SYSTEM

The least-used system of performance counseling—yet potentially one of the most valuable—is self-evaluation. It is based on the assumption that the employee knows more than anyone else about her or his needs, wants, abilities, motivation, and aspirations. This system, used in conjunction with another, can be a powerful tool for both the employee and the organization.

The employee's self-evaluation can be made verbally, in writing, or through the preparation of a portfolio. With the verbal method, the employee simply states her daily or weekly progress as she perceives it. The leader may ask, for example, "What have you done today (or this week) that you are proud of?" Or, "What would you do differently if you had the day (or week) to do over?"

The employee submits a report describing her progress in words or using a checklist of tasks completed or skills achieved. The leader also completes a written report and then holds a conference with the employee. (More information about the steps in holding a work performance conference is given later in this chapter.)

In the portfolio method, the employee assembles a collection of work samples. Examples include photographs of a project at various stages of completion, samples of items made or created, copies of reports or articles written, and transcripts of speeches delivered. The employee can then show her boss her accomplishments at periodic performance reviews and can substantiate a request for a promotion or raise. She can also use the portfolio when looking for a new job.

The self-evaluative system has several benefits. First, it encourages a collaborative relationship between leader and follower. Second, the leader obtains concrete information for assessing the employee's work performance and readiness for advancement. Third, the employee has a complete, ongoing record of her accomplishments to present to others who need to assess her strengths. Finally, the conference review reinforces the employee's sense of worth and thus provides an incentive for growth.

The major drawback to the self-evaluative system is that careful preparation is required. Also, since most workers are unfamiliar with it, they will need to be instructed in its purpose and in how to make fair and accurate self-assessments. People tend to judge themselves more harshly than others do. Employees must be encouraged to balance self-criticism with self-praise.

The performance counseling cycle

The activities involved in performance counseling include acquiring knowledge about the organization and the employee, preparing for the counseling session, holding the conference, reaching an agreement with the employee, and monitoring the employee's progress. These five activities are cyclical, as Figure 7 shows.

Knowledge. Performance counseling begins with knowledge about the organization. As a leader, you should be fully aware of the goals of the organization, the part your work unit plays in it, and how each of your followers' jobs fits into the whole. It is your responsibility to know job demands and expectations well enough to explain them to employees.

You also need knowledge about each employee. This information can be obtained through the Hersey-Blanchard "Maturity Scale" (see Chapter 5), through conversations with the employee, and through observations of the employee's work, attitudes, abilities, and values.

Figure 7. The performance counseling cycle.

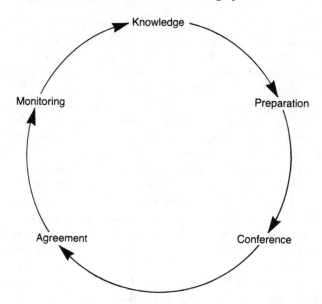

Preparation. Preparation involves establishing a climate conducive to productive counseling and devising measurement tools for the conferences. As noted earlier, in order to establish an atmosphere of trust, you must model those behaviors you expect in others and display a willingness to explore new ideas and values without passing judgment. Remember, too, that the conferences should be held in privacy and comfort so that employees feel "safe." Prepare your employees for the conference by making them aware of its purpose, time, and place. If they are participating in self-evaluation, give them lead time to complete their self-assessment.

Your next task is to determine which method of performance counseling to use. If a standard evaluation procedure has been set by organizational policy or union contract, you may not have a choice. However, you can modify or add to the assessment process. If, for instance, you are required to complete and file a standard checklist, you can attach a written report explaining your assessment. You can also ask the employee to complete a self-evaluation checklist before the conference and to be prepared to talk about the items.

If you choose to modify your organization's standard evaluation procedure, be sure to check with the manager responsible for developing performance appraisal systems. Make sure you have a clear rationale for your modifications and can explain how they benefit both the organization and the employee. Your main argument may be that a

thorough assessment of work performance leads to increased productivity.

Conference. At the conference, make the employee feel as comfortable as possible. Arrange the room so that both of you will be at ease,
with no desks or tables between you to create nonverbal barriers. Make
sure you will not be interrupted by visitors or telephone calls. Try to
relieve any anxiety on the part of the employee. At the beginning of the
conference, ask the employee outright, "How are you feeling about this
conference?" Talking about these feelings can ease discomfort.

Give the employee the chance to talk first. This will indicate that
you value the employee's assessment of her progress, needs, skills, and
goals. For example, open with the question, "What progress do you feel
you've made since we last talked about your work performance?" or
"How do you assess your performance in the tasks for which you are
responsible?" Your role at this time is to *listen* and *clarify*. Your
comments should be aimed only at helping the employee understand
her thinking and feelings. When the employee has finished, proceed
with your review.

Agreement. After both reviews have been presented, you are ready
to reach an agreement. It is important that you explain any aspects of
the job that are beyond the employee's control—such as work hours or
the completion of certain forms—so that she knows what areas cannot
be negotiated. Explain the rationale behind these organizational norms
or procedures.

Work with the employee to identify areas needing attention. For
instance, if the employee has had problems arriving to work on time,
explore why she is late so often. After discussing possible causes, help
the employee find reasonable solutions to the problem. Throughout the
process, continue to uphold organizational expectations, but do not
ignore the employee's individual problems and needs.

Carefully explore each problem until you reach a resolution. When
you are done, prepare a performance planning worksheet (**#21**), listing
the major activities or skills the employee will deal with during a set
period of time. State specifically what will be done, how, by whom, and
when. This planning procedure involves shared responsibility: The
employee is to accomplish certain tasks or make certain changes while
you, as leader, are to provide the training, resources, and guidance the
employee needs. Both you and the employee should sign the agreement
and keep a copy for your files.

Monitoring. As the leader, you are responsible for monitoring the
employee's progress and renewing the counseling cycle at specified
times. For instance, if you decide that a weekly 15-minute conference
would be helpful, it is your responsibility to arrange it. This responsibility must be taken seriously. If you forget or decide you have more

21   PLANNING FOR PERFORMANCE

_____   _____
Employee   Supervisor/Manager

I. We agree that the following progress has been made since _____.

II. Planning for future growth:

Activity/Skill	Behavioral change	How will this be accomplished?	By whom?	When?
1. _____	_____	_____	_____	____
2. _____	_____	_____	_____	____
3. _____	_____	_____	_____	____
4. _____	_____	_____	_____	____
5. _____	_____	_____	_____	____

III. We agree that we will monitor the progress of this plan on _____.

_____   _____   _____
Signature   Date   Signature

important things to do at that time, you risk losing the employee's trust.

Counseling your followers to enhance their personal and professional growth can benefit you, your followers, and your organization. The care, thought, and time you invest in the process will pay dividends in more effective leadership.

REFERENCES

1. Harvey Jackins, *The Human Side of Human Beings: The Theory of Reevaluation Counseling* (Seattle: Rationale Island Publishers, 1972).
2. Gail Sheehy, *Passages: Predictable Crises of Adult Life* (New York: Bantam Books, 1977).

RESOURCES

Career Counseling and Life Planning

Bolles, Richard Nelson. *What Color Is Your Parachute? A Practical Manual for Job Hunters and Career Changers.* Berkeley, CA: Ten Speed Press, 1978.
O'Neill, Nena, and George O'Neill. *Shifting Gears.* New York: McGraw-Hill, 1974.
Scholz, Nelle, Judith Prince, and Gordon Miller. *How to Decide: A Guide for Women.* New York: College Entrance Examination Board, 1975.

Performance Counseling

Connellan, Thomas. *How to Improve Human Performance: Behaviorism in Business and Industry.* New York: Harper & Row, 1977.
Harrison, Jared F. *Improving Performance and Productivity (Why Won't They Do What I Want Them to Do?).* Reading, MA: Addison-Wesley, 1978.
Kirschenbaum, Howard, Sidney Simon, and Rodney Napie. *Wad-Ja-Get? The Grading Game in American Education.* New York: Hart Publishing Co., 1971.
Luthans, Fred, and Robert Kreitner. *Organizational Behavior Modification.* Glenview, IL: Scott Foresman, 1975.
Mager, Robert, and Peter Pipe. *Analyzing Performance Problems, or "You Really Oughta Wanna."* Belmont, CA: Fearon-Pittman, 1974.
Simon, Sidney, and James Bellanca, eds. *Degrading the Grading Myths: A Primer of Alternatives to Grades and Marks.* Washington, D.C.: Association for Supervision and Curriculum Development, 1976.
Simon, Sidney. *Negative Criticism.* Niles, IL: Argus Communications, 1978.

Personal Counseling

Argyris, Chris. "Explorations in Consulting-Client Relationships." *Human Organization*, Vol. 20, No. 3, pp. 121–133.
Combs, Arthur, Donald Avila, and William Purkey. *Helping Relationships: Basic Concepts of the Helping Professions.* Boston: Allyn and Bacon, 1972.
Jackins, Harvey. *The Human Side of Human Beings: The Theory of Reevaluation Counseling.* Seattle: Rationale Island Publishers, 1972.
Jackins, Harvey. *The Human Situation.* Seattle: Rationale Island Publishers, 1975.
Rogers, Carl R. *On Becoming a Person.* Boston: Houghton Mifflin, 1961.

7

Skills in management science

IN AN INDUSTRIAL AGE, the application of scientific principles to the study of management functions was inevitable. Following World War II emphasis was placed on quantitatively prescribing how organizational goals and activities should be carried out. Thus management science was born. Dealing with techniques, mechanics, and tools rather than principles, researchers in management science were concerned with two basic types of skills: those dealing with procedures and those dealing with people. Chart #22 outlines the activities involved.

"Procedures" skills focus on the organizational aspects of management. They include the routine application of various types of business controls, such as cost accounting, inventory maintenance, payment of salaries, preparation of budgets, quality control, problem identification, time management, and analysis of procedures. "People" skills include controlling or monitoring the implementation of tasks, developing the potential of employees, evaluating their progress, solving problems, and setting objectives. As you study the management science chart, notice that a majority of the activities are carried out by the middle manager.

Management science focuses on the efficient accomplishment of organizational goals and objectives. It is important, however, for the management scientist to keep a clear perspective on "efficiency." The tools of management science are powerful; their wrong or careless use can do serious harm to both the organization and the employee. While increased efficiency is desirable, it must be achieved with an awareness and appreciation of human needs. The leader must strive to balance the goals of the organization with those of the individual. Management

22 MANAGEMENT SCIENCE SKILLS

	First-line/Low	Middle	Top	Executive
Procedures Organizing		• Writes job descriptions and qualifications • Organizes work and group activities • Formulates wage and salary plans • Develops budget	• Applies time management techniques • Manages changes • Manages differences and resolves conflicts	• Establishes organizational structure, chart, and roles of personnel • Initiates review of organization's direction
People Controlling	• Monitors performance daily	• Establishes reporting system • Develops performance standards • Measures results against plans • Takes corrective action • Maintains proper inventories		
Development	• Recommends employees for training	• Selects and trains new employees • Assesses need for training and development programs • Establishes, carries out programs	• Develops performance appraisal system • Determines promotability	• Formulates and approves executive development
Evaluation	• Evaluates results daily	• Analyzes, appraises, and interprets performance results • Recommends new procedures and processes to top executive	• Evaluates new ideas	
Problem solving	• Resolves urgent and pending problems	• Interprets and utilizes information system • Identifies problems • Solves immediate problems • Develops criteria for success • Generates and analyzes alternate solutions	• Identifies potential problems	
Setting objectives		• Sets goals and priorities • Utilizes systems such as MBO		• Reviews alternative methods to set goals and objectives • Sets long-term objectives

science activities are tools of analysis; they represent means to an end, not ends in themselves. Put another way, efficiency is a way to accomplish goals, but is not in itself a goal.

Assessing Your Management Science Skills

You now have the opportunity to assess your management science skills. Decide if you want to focus on improving skills at your current leadership position or on developing skills for the level above you. Review chart #22 to determine which skills you already possess. Rate these strengths with the following code:

+3   Highly developed
+2   Somewhat developed
+1   Minimally developed

For instance, if you have had some experience in selecting and orienting employees, but only in collaboration with your immediate supervisor, you might rate yourself +2.

Next, review the chart to identify those skills you would like to develop more fully. Use a similar rating system:

−1   Needs minimal development
−2   Needs some development
−3   Needs considerable development

For instance, if your attempts to use your time effectively seem to fall short and you have trouble getting things done on time, a rating of −2 would probably be appropriate to your situation. List the skills that need the most development on the planning sheet in chart #23, under the column marked "Skills I want to develop." Number those listed in the order in which you want to develop them.

This chapter deals exclusively with time management, emphasizing the management of both your professional and personal life. Additional, related skills are presented in other chapters: problem solving in Chapter 8, evaluation techniques in Chapter 6, and conflict resolution in Chapter 4. On your planning sheet, identify resources from this book and elsewhere that you can use to develop skills not covered here.

Perceptions of Time

Experience shows that most time is wasted, not in hours, but in minutes. A bucket with a small hole in the bottom gets just as empty as the bucket that is deliberately kicked over.

Skills I want to develop	Order of development	Found in chapter	Additional resources

Time is everywhere—supposedly readily available, yet often difficult to find. Time is an integral concern in our culture, as indicated by numerous adages:

"Time flies."
"Time is money."
"A stitch in time saves nine."
"There's no time like the present."
"Time waits for no person."

All kinds of devices are available as reminders of the time. How many watches do you own? Do you always wear one? In which rooms of your house do you have clocks? Which have bells or chimes? Some people have several clocks in the same room! Do you refer to these time devices often? Or do others have to remind you of the time? "Ms. Jones, it's time for your next appointment." "Mother, it's time for my dinner." "We don't have enough time to finish this up before lunch."

Time influences nearly every aspect of people's lives. As a professional interested in effective leadership, you are most likely concerned about the best way to use your time. You may feel that time controls you or that you do not have enough time to do the things you would like.

Time management is an increasingly important concern in our complex society, and several excellent books have been written about it. However, like most management books, they were written by men and thus reflect masculine attitudes and perceptions. This chapter examines time management from a woman's viewpoint and emphasizes her unique need to balance time between professional and personal demands.

Anne Wilson Schaef of the Women's Institute of Alternative Psychotherapy of Boulder, Colorado, distinguishes between the way time is perceived by the "white male system" and by those not included in that system, such as women, blacks, Latinos, and native Americans.[1] She observes that those who operate in the dominant white male system see time as an absolute. That is, all behaviors and activities are measured by an external clock; such people are either "late," "early," or "on time."

To other people, however, time is seen as part of a process, a total experience. In other words, behaviors and activities are measured by a highly developed "internal clock" of subjective time. For example, in the native American culture, people show up for a meeting when they show up because what is occurring at a particular moment is more important than an obligation to be somewhere else "on time." Blacks who have not adopted the white male time system operate on what is referred to as "black time," which means 15 to 30 minutes later than what the clock registers. Women who grow up in a particular ethnic or racial group often retain attitudes toward time that reflect that group. Most white women, especially those in the working world, however, have internalized the white male system.

A study done at Purdue University shows that people whose internal clocks are synchronized with actual timepieces score well on tests designed to evaluate personal drive and the ability to solve problems and accomplish tasks. Other studies show that a good sense of time is related to a realistic outlook on life.[2]

What happens to those people who operate according to an internal clock while the organization in which they work operates according to an external one? Usually, those in the minority are expected to adjust their behaviors to fit the dominant culture's norms—that is, to be on time as measured by the clock. Those who do not adjust are judged harshly or disciplined. Rarely do members of the dominant group attempt to understand the attitudes and behaviors of those who hold a different view of time.

What can be done? Women and minorities need to recapture the usefulness of their own time systems and examine their own behaviors according to their needs—as they determine them and not only as others define them.

The juggling act

Women are keenly aware of time—its scarcity and its use. They constantly wrestle with a uniquely female phenomenon—the juggling of time to accommodate various personal and professional demands.

With the rapid increase of women in the labor market, through economic need or desire for achievement, more and more women must face the "juggling act." Whether a woman works full time or part time, she frequently finds all her personal time taken up by the endless activities of parenting, cleaning, cooking, washing, mending, and shopping. As Letty Pogrebin points out, women are now expected to want "everything"—career, marriage, and children.[3] Fulfillment through a career is accepted and even encouraged as long as marriage and children are also part of a woman's life scheme. This has serious implications for the working woman, who must keep a running list of family errands to be done, call home about a sick child, or arrange for dental appointments, all while she is working. Men don't do this. When they are at work, they focus on their jobs. Why the difference? Women are taught that it is their responsibility to attend to the needs of others, so if they choose to work, they simply add that to their family responsibilities.

Working, then, adds to a woman's already long list of responsibilities. What can you as a woman do about this juggling act? The time
management techniques outlined in this chapter are not designed to
help you manage "everything." They are intended to help you explore
and organize what you want out of life—and to set priorities—so that
you do not become a casualty of professional and personal pressures.
Accepting the belief that more is better often carries the price tag of
high blood pressure and heart attacks. If you are willing to give up
being Wonder Woman, read on.

Setting Goals for the Use of Your Time

The first step in managing time effectively is to identify what you want
from life. The clearer your philosophy and goals are, the easier it will
be to make daily decisions on how to organize and spend your time.
The review of your lifetime goals in Chapter 1 was the first step to a
saner life.

Vivian, for example, leads a whirlwind life. Her professional
activities keep her going from early morning to late evening, and she
works two Saturdays a month. As a result, she has little social life. When
she reviewed her lifetime goals, she recognized that her major goal was
to develop her professional career. As a result, she decided not to try to
do everything. Although she must devote the bulk of her time to her
work, she now arranges to spend time with her friends on alternate
Saturdays so that she no longer feels guilty about not socializing. If
friends suggest activities that don't fit into her scheme, she tells them
about her plans for the use of her time.

As a city planner, Ina never seemed to find time to write up the
ideas collecting in her head and in her files. Ina reviewed her lifetime
goals and reaffirmed her desire to influence the field of urban
development. Recognizing writing as an effective means to convey her
ideas and publishing as a means to build her professional credibility,
Ina decided to reorganize her life to allow some time for writing every
week. With the aid of a few time management techniques, Ina was able
to set aside half a day each week for writing. Her secretary handles all
interruptions and calls and makes no appointments during that time.

In both cases, Vivian and Ina have made an effort to determine the
direction of their lives and have decided to use their limited time to
achieve their dreams. How do you spend your time? In chart **#24**
estimate how much time you spend on various activities. Add up the
amount of time you spend in each category and calculate the percentage of your total time (24 hours) it represents.

Now draw two "circles of life" like those in Figure 8. One should

24   TIME ASSESSMENT CHART

Activities	Weekdays	Weekends
Essential activities		
Eating		
Sleeping		
Routine activities		
At work		
In personal life		
Working		
Paid job		
Community activities		
Housework		
Relationships		
Professional		
Family		
Friends		
Relatives		
Solitary activities		
Reading		
Writing		
Physical activities		
Outdoors		
Indoors		
Totals		

Figure 8. Circles of life.

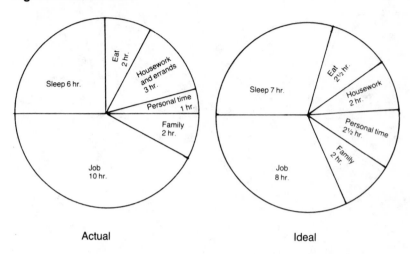

Actual

Ideal

represent how you presently spend your time. From this you can determine if you spend time in the best way for you. Which activities take up more time than necessary? Over which areas do you have more control? In which categories do you want to increase or decrease the amount of time spent? The other circle should reflect your lifetime goals and values and how you'd like to spend your time.

Now repeat the previous two steps, but focus only on the time you spend at work. First list your essential activities (the major tasks for which you are responsible) and then your routine activities (phone calls, outlining tasks for your secretary, reading mail). Next, convert this information into two "circles of worklife." The first should describe how you currently spend your work time and the second how you would need to organize your time to incorporate your values and lifetime goals. Figure 9 illustrates a school principal's assessment.

Remember that you have only a set amount of time available—24 hours. While this cannot be changed, the amount of time you spend on some activities can be. If, for instance, you want to increase your sleep time, your solitary time, or your social activities time, you must decrease your number of work, home, or errand hours.

The school principal described above decided to work 9 rather than 11 hours to increase her time for personal activities. In addition, she decided that she spent too much time attending meetings, dealing with correspondence, and talking on the phone. By scaling down these activities, she gained time for the more important activities of talking, revising and writing curricula, planning, reading, and taking lunch breaks—while maintaining the important time for student contact.

Figure 9. Circles of worklife.

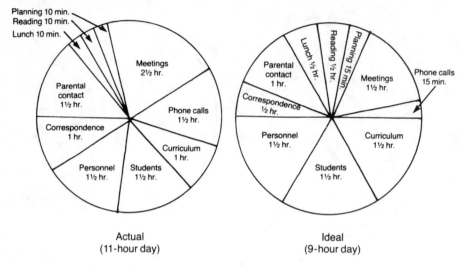

Actual
(11-hour day)

Ideal
(9-hour day)

Establishing Priorities

Probably the most difficult aspect of managing time is accepting the real control you have over it. Women often surrender personal control and power by believing that others have the right to demand their time and by imagining catastrophic results if they refuse to be interrupted. Begin thinking and acting with this new direction: "I am in charge of my life and my time."

Women who want to do and be "everything" have a difficult time setting priorities. Because they want to do so much—at once and on time—they never finish. They do not see that some work doesn't need immediate attention—at least by them.

This section outlines a technique to help you set priorities on the use of your time so you can focus on the activities you value most. The system helps you rank according to importance every task at work and at home— each phone call, request for help, errand, report or item to be read, piece of mail.

The system, devised by Alan Lakein, involves an "ABC" approach to ranking activities.[4] At the moment a task appears you decide whether, relative to other demands, it is of utmost priority (A), of secondary importance (B), or of least importance (C). In this way, you sort out tasks so that the most important reach the top and the rest lie low until they become important enough to require attention. If you delay your ABC decision, all tasks will seem important—but they cannot all be equally important at the same time. With the ABC method, you decide what tasks are most important and concentrate on those, accepting that many C items may be left indefinitely.

Make two lists of all the tasks hanging over you at the moment—one for those in your professional life and one for those in your personal life. Review your lists and assign an A, B, or C to each item. Be sure to use all three letters in your lists so that all tasks are not given high priority. Next, get three boxes or files and label them A, B, and C. File any paper or other tangible evidence of each task—whether it is a phone call, report, project, or errand—into its appropriate box. Write down and file those tasks without tangible reminders to be sure they will not be forgotten.

A word of reassurance: No important task ever gets lost or forgotten in B or C files. It tends to rise to the surface, become an A task—as its urgency increases.

At this point, focus on the items in your A box and ignore the others. Because you can't do everything in box A at once, you will have to set priorities for these activities. Re-sort items in Box A in their order of importance. Or make a list of the items and assign numbers to them (A-1, A-2, A-3, and so forth).

Taking Time to Plan

Setting aside time to plan—even ten minutes a day—is one of the best investments you can make. Some people like to plan their activities for the next day or week before the close of the day or week; others like to plan at the beginning of each day or week. When you do it is not as important as the fact that you do it.

An organized plan tells you which activities need to be done each day or week. Rather than worry about the tasks planned in three weeks, you can focus on the most important tasks of the moment. Review what has been done so that you can set appropriate goals for the day. Planning the use of your time assures that you do the most important tasks first, that your activities fit in with your goals, and that you gain a sense of accomplishment as each step is completed.

Your goal in planning is to arrange your time to accommodate both your immediate needs and your long-term objectives. As you set priorities for your activities (whether you use the ABC method or some other system), ask yourself: "How urgent is this task now? How does it help me achieve my lifetime goal?"

As you plan your daily schedule, group similar kinds of activities. Then try to accomplish them within a block of time rather than spreading them out. For instance, return all your phone calls at the same time. If someone isn't in, indicate the hours you can receive a return call so that you aren't constantly interrupted. Devote an entire day to meetings if necessary. Block out a few hours for reading reports and journals, for planning a project, or for writing. Fragmenting the day with many different activities often creates a frantic pace and can lead you to delay more involved tasks.

Stay in touch with how and when you work best. Listen to your internal clock. Some people are most productive in the morning, some in the afternoon, and some at night. It is important to identify your own energy cycle—over the course of a day or a week—and to use it to your advantage. Determine the best time to talk on the phone, hold meetings, run errands, read, write, plan, exercise, eat, meditate, or be with your loved ones and friends.

My internal clock, for example, tells me that I am a morning person; I have little energy after 3:30. I capitalize on my cycle with the following system: I do my writing and creative program development in the morning. I can't operate effectively with interruption, so during this time I transfer all phone calls to my answering machine or have my secretary take them. Colleagues and friends know I will return their calls after 12:00. I hold business meetings and return calls during lunch or in the afternoon and do all my errands in one session. I save socializing for my low-energy times because it demands less creativity, and in fact can be reenergizing.

Handling Interruptions

How often have others asked you, "Do you have a minute?" A ringing phone symbolizes this request. Of course, some people don't ask, they just interrupt. Dealing with interruptions and the unexpected is crucial to effective time management. Think about any one day and the number of interruptions you had. Who initiated them? When did they occur? What did you do?

In the past, when others interrupted me at a moment when I didn't want to be disturbed, I would accept the interruption, give half of my attention to the new interaction, and resent it for the duration. Now, I either ignore the interruption (don't answer the phone or door) or hold it off (explain that I'm involved and will return the call or answer the question in 15 minutes), and return to my other activity.

You do not have to be a slave to the telephone, the doorbell, children with questions, or husbands with indirect requests for attention. Women must learn that they have the right to determine the use of their time and to say no. Even at the risk of being called selfish, inflexible, unresponsive, or unloving, they must assert this right.

Regardless of what others think, women must break the socialization patterns that teach them to put the needs of others before their own.

How often have you wished for one hour of uninterrupted time to read, think, take a walk, or do anything that gives you pleasure? Women who complain that this is not possible are often to blame for not arranging uninterrupted time for themselves—and, in fact, often "train" those around them to interrupt. When a woman is interrupted and says nothing, she reinforces the interrupter's right to interrupt. If children, for example, are allowed to interrupt their mother at work when they've been told to direct all requests to their father during that time, they will continue to do so. If the husband calls with "a quick question" and the wife says nothing about the interruption, he may interpret her acceptance of his call as an indication that her work is not important and can be interrupted.

At home or at work, you must learn to control interruptions. First be clear with yourself about what you expect from others. Decide when you are willing to be interrupted and let others know what you expect from them. For example, at your office, have your secretary hold all interruptions until a certain time, or indicate which calls you will accept. Then stick to your decision. At home, if you've arranged for a quiet hour behind closed doors, don't budge or accept interruptions.

What if your job requires you to accept any and all interruptions? Like other helping professionals, school principals protest vehemently that they must be available at *all* times to parents, staff, and students. Have you ever felt the same way about your job? People who feel this way tend to believe in two tenets: (1) they must serve others constantly or be judged as insensitive ("How can you be a human person and say 'no' to others?"), and (2) if they aren't constantly involved, things will fall apart ("I can't afford to be sick; they never do it right"). In reality, leaders whose jobs involve a great deal of contact with others do not have to be available 100 percent of the time. "Emergencies" are in the eye of the beholder; each individual perceives her case to be crucial and to need immediate action. Dire consequences seldom result from delayed attention. Emergencies such as fires, natural disasters, violent acts, and accidents are, of course, exceptions. But how many "perceived" emergencies actually demand immediate attention? Probably very few.

You, as a leader, need to understand that each request or interruption is not an emergency and does not need immediate attention—at least by you. Teach those around you to sort out that which does and does not demand interruption and assign them the responsibility of handling tasks while you are unavailable. Delegation, of course, implies that you accept their handling of the situation in *their* way, even if it differs from yours.

Getting Others Involved

Deciding that you can't and won't do everything means that you must get others involved in accomplishing tasks. The skills of delegating tasks to others in a work setting are examined in Chapter 5. This section focuses on the art of delegation in your personal life, describing a "cooperative living" system that my family and I developed. This system enabled me to give up being Super Mom and got my entire family involved.

The Hart Plan

In 1972, at the age of 31, I was still relatively new into an exploration of my skills, needs, and awareness as a woman. My husband and I had just moved into our first house and had gotten a dog for our sons, Chris and Rich. I had started graduate school full time. Within two weeks, I found myself assuming all the family responsibilities. No one had told me to; it was simply assumed that I had time to do these tasks, since I was "just a student." We had a family crisis because I was feeling used and angry.

My husband, Arn, and I decided that this could not go on. He agreed that all the work was not just mine to cope with. After considering several possibilities, we decided that our boys, then 9 and 11, were old enough to learn many of the household tasks necessary for our existence. We also wanted our boys to leave home as fully functioning adults, capable of taking care of themselves and thus more likely to work cooperatively with any other people they might live with.

We divided all tasks into seven categories: food, housecleaning, clothing, transportation, children, home care, and finances. We then prepared a checklist (**#25**) of the routine tasks that needed to be done within each category. Next, we held a family conference. Each of us picked our first choice. After all first choices were identified and assigned, we moved to our second choices. As we progressed, we discovered that no one wanted to do any of the housecleaning. We continued the negotiations until even that chore was taken care of. The assignments were posted so that everyone would know her or his role and disputes over responsibilities could be settled.

What were the results? First, as parents, we had to be very patient for several years as the boys learned to do their jobs effectively. Rich, for example, had chosen to do the laundry. He had to learn how to sort the clothes by color and type, to use correct soaps and additives, to request laundry supplies from the "shopper," and to hang up clothes when they came out of the dryer so ironing was unnecessary.

Second, we discovered that everyone now had a stake in the

Food
Purchase
Weekly
Emergency

Preparation
Weekdays
Weekends
Parties

Cleanup
Breakfast
Lunch
Dinner
Parties

Feed pets

Children
Help with schoolwork
Attend school functions
Parent/teacher conferences
Read to children
Bath
Bedtime
Arrange for child care

Home care
Lawn mowing
Flowers
Major repairs
Minor repairs

Clothing
Purchasing
Washing
Ironing
Mending
Dry cleaning

Transportation
Purchase gas
Change oil
Arrange for maintenance
Arrange for insurance

Finances
Keep accounts
Pay bills
Arrange for insurance
Invest money

Housecleaning
By room
Kitchen
Living room
Bathroom(s)
Bedrooms
Garage
Basement
Hallways

By function
Dusting
Vacuuming
Floor waxing
Wall scrubbing

operation of our home. We began to hear comments like "Who messed up the sink I just cleaned?" and "If you don't put the item on the shopping list, I don't know you need it." The kids in the neighborhood learned that on certain nights our boys had to leave their play early to help their father with dinner.

Third, we learned that contracts must be renegotiated as people's needs change. We have made several contractual adjustments over the years to meet our interests, lifestyle, and activities. When Chris complained that he was doing more than his brother, we calculated the time each of us spent on our chores. We not only found that Chris did put in more time than Rich, but also discovered that Arn was putting in proportionately more time than the rest of us, since he was in charge of grocery shopping and all meal preparation. The contract was renegotiated in each case.

Finally, we found that our contract handled the routine tasks but did not account for occasional or unexpected tasks. These included responding to the notice for the dog's heartworm test or dentist appointments, arranging for routine maintenance and emergency repairs on our cars, attending parent–teacher conferences, buying gifts for relatives, and answering grandparents' letters. Once again, we learned that men and women had been trained to respond in different ways. As a woman, I had assumed responsibility for keeping track of all these extra tasks. I either did them myself or arranged to get them done. Arn had been trained not to notice that they needed doing. He now makes an effort to be more aware of what needs doing and I stop myself from automatically doing what I see needs doing. Unlearning these socialization patterns is difficult, but rewarding.

Cooperative living

What can you do to get others involved? First, identify the tasks that need to be done both routinely and sporadically. Second, learn how other families share work. Many magazines feature articles on "cooperative living" arrangements. Ask friends and acquaintances how they manage their lives. Explore as many models as you can to find the best plan for you.

Third, appeal to those you live with to cooperate in this venture. Even small children need to be included in the plan. Your partner may or may not accept the idea of dividing responsibilities. Some men refuse outright ("If you want to work, fine, but you are still responsible for the children and for hot meals on the table at 6:00 P.M."). Other men give the illusion of cooperation but in reality are not complete believers in the system ("Of course I'd be willing to do some of *your* errands *for* you").

Indirectly noncooperative behavior can be difficult to contend with because it is often hard to find concrete evidence of nonsupport. Many women begin to wonder about their own perceptions ("Perhaps he is being cooperative and I'm crazy to ask for more"). Your success in reaching such a partner depends on the willingness of both of you to root out the source of the problem and to seek alternative solutions.

Overtly noncooperative behavior may be easier to spot, but it is often impossible to change. In this case, a woman isn't fighting an illusion. She may have to leave the unhealthy situation rather than deny her basic right to cooperation. In most cases, as you demand more cooperation, you can expect conflict. As Jean Baker Miller points out, women as a group have been able to deal with conflict only indirectly because "it is practically impossible to initiate open conflict when you are *totally* dependent on the other person or group for the basic materials and psychological means of existence."[5]

How does a woman gain more cooperation from those around her—her partner, children, or other adults? Usually with a great deal of effort and persistence! You must be clear on your basic rights and express them to others—often and over and over again. You can also appeal to their self-interest. Demonstrate how their cooperation can benefit them directly and indirectly. For instance, if you are less tired from overwork, you will be more cheerful and pleasant to live with. Point out how your pay check enriches their material existence. Reassure them that you will help them learn how to handle additional tasks around the house so they will not be left to their own devices.

Skills in communication and human relations (Chapters 3 and 4) can help you deal with these problems. But the foundation is your own philosophy—that you are in charge of your life and your time and that you do not have to do *everything*. This philosophy will lead you to a more fulfilling life.

REFERENCES

1. Anne Wilson Schaef, "It's Not Necessary to Deny Another's Reality in Order to Affirm Your Own—The Systematization of Dualism in the White Male Structure," First National Conference on Human Relations in Education, June 18–22, 1978.
2. "The Different Ways We Perceive Time," *State Journal*, April 2, 1978.
3. Letty Pogrebin, "Can Women Really Have It All?" *MS*, March 1978, p. 47.
4. Alan Lakein, *How to Get Control of Your Time and Your Life* (New York: New American Library, 1973), pp. 63–68.
5. Jean Baker Miller, *Toward a New Psychology of Women* (Boston: Beacon Press, 1976), p. 127.

RESOURCES

Goldfein, Donna. *Every Woman's Guide to Time Management.* Milbrae, CA: Les Femmes, 1977.

Lakein, Alan. *The Time of Your Life.* New York: New American Library, 1973.

MacKenzie, Alec R. *The Time Trap: Managing Your Way Out.* La Jolla, CA: University Associates, 1972.

Miller, Jean Baker. *Toward a New Psychology of Women.* Boston: Beacon Press, 1976.

Pogrebin, Letty. "Can Women Really Have It All?" *MS*, March 1978, p. 47.

Pogrebin, Letty. *Getting Yours.* New York: David McKay, 1975. Chapters 6 and 7.

Williams, Marcille Gray. *The New Executive Woman.* Radnor, PA: Chilton Book Company, 1977. Chapter 14.

8

Delving into decisions

WHAT KINDS of decisions do you make? How do you feel about making them? Is it easy or difficult? What do you need to know about decision making to become a more effective leader?

The Buck Stops Here

In every setting, *someone* must make the decisions. In organizations, leaders have this responsibility and therefore need to understand the kinds of decisions made at different levels in the organization. They need to know that decision making requires a knowledge of the total organization, the people involved, the time restraints, and the complexity of the problem. In addition, leaders should be aware of the relationship between risk taking and decision making and of how men's and women's different perceptions of this relationship affect their leadership styles.

Decision-making activities vary according to the type of problem to be solved. Chart #26 shows how decision making changes with the leader's level in the organization. The first two rows in the chart describe the nature of the decisions made at each level. The third row outlines the processes involved. As you can see, the supervisor is involved in more concrete, pragmatic, and short-term decisions, whereas the executive is involved in more abstract, holistic, and long-term decisions.

Studies have shown that women usually focus their attention on details, whereas men tend to focus on the whole. Thus women are

26 DECISION-MAKING SKILLS

	First-line	Low	Middle	Top/Executive
Content of decisions	Concrete and pragmatic Pertaining to work unit		Practical application of abstract to operational procedures	Abstract, strategic, and complex Pertaining to the whole organization
Time frame	Makes short-term, immediate decisions		Reviews long-term impact of decisions	Makes long-term decisions
Process	• Assigns workers to particular job • Carries out decisions	• Understands and uses selected decision-making processes • Seeks advice from superiors regarding decisions • Follows standardized procedures	• Selects appropriate decision-making processes • Determines degrees of participation by subordinates • Leads group discussions	• Establishes effective decision-making climate • Facilitates decision-making group discussions and meetings • Analyzes potential impact of decisions on the future • Exercises final authority on decisions

generally effective in making day-to-day, short-term decisions but often have difficulty with long-term decisions dealing with the organization's structure, goals, policies, and procedures.

If women want to move out of first-line and low-level supervisory positions and into middle and top management, they must learn to incorporate a long-term outlook into their leadership style.

The leader at higher levels needs to know a variety of decision-making and problem-solving methods. As you explore the methods outlined in this chapter, keep in mind that your approach to taking risks interacts with your decision-making skills. Chapter 10 explores risk-taking skills and planning for future risks. You may want to read the appropriate section of that chapter as you work on your decision-making skills.

As noted earlier, women have been socialized to seek approval from others, particularly from men. Their behavior and feelings of self-worth are frequently based on this approval. Difficulty arises, then, when women must make decisions (short- or long-term, simple or complex) that jeopardize the approval they have been trained to seek. Often women will make no decision, waiting until all bases are covered, or change a decision unnecessarily. Such behaviors are inappropriate for leaders. Women must learn to take the risks involved in making decisions.

Assessing Your Decision-Making Skills

It's time to make some decisions. As before, you need to determine whether you want to focus on improving skills for your current leadership position or on developing skills for the level above you. Review chart #26 to determine which skills you already possess. Rate these strengths with the following code:

> +3   Highly developed
> +2   Somewhat developed
> +1   Minimally developed

For instance, if you are quite familiar with various problem-solving methods and have used them regularly, you might rate yourself +2 or +3.

Next, review the chart to identify those skills you'd like to develop more fully. Use a similar rating system:

> −1   Needs minimal development
> −2   Needs some development
> −3   Needs considerable development

For instance, if you learned a problem-solving method at a training program but have had little opportunity to practice it, you might rate yourself − 1.

List the skills that need development on the planning sheet in chart **#27,** under the column marked "Skills I want to develop." Number these skills in the order you would like to develop them.

This chapter covers the following aspects of decision making:

1. Who to involve in making the decision.
2. Voting and consensus methods.
3. Elements of the decision-making process.
4. The Compact Problem-Solving Process.
5. The Comprehensive Problem-Solving Process.

Mark on the appropriate column the skills covered in this chapter. List any additional resources available to you.

Who Should Be Involved in Making the Decision

Can you remember when, as a leader, you alone made a decision that should have involved others? Can you remember when you had useful ideas about some decision your boss had to make but were not asked to contribute or were not taken seriously?

Deciding who should be involved in the decision-making process is difficult because the variables change with each new problem. Six considerations are involved in deciding who to involve in a particular decision-making process:

Authority
Experience
Education
Timing
Motivation
Climate

Authority, education, and experience

Do you personally have the authority to make the decision? If so, how explicitly has your authority been defined? If not, who has the authority to make the decision? How much related experience and education do you have to solve the problem?

When you are low on authority, experience, and education, ask

27   PLANNING SHEET FOR SKILLS IN DECISION MAKING

Skills I want to develop	Order of development	Found in chapter	Additional resources

those who *do* have them to help you make the decision. But when you do meet these three criteria, act on them. Women leaders often hesitate in this situation because they perceive possible loss of approval as too great a risk. To be effective leaders, women must consciously learn to weigh the potential gains against the potential losses, instead of focusing only on the latter. As women learn the skills of risk taking, they increasingly recognize that they have a broad base of experience to draw upon in making decisions.

A leader's ability to make decisions is based in part on her position in the organization. Because women have held relatively powerless social and professional positions, they are frequently unfamiliar and uncomfortable with power and thus fail to utilize it effectively. Explore your feelings about power and consider situations in which using your power would be appropriate. As your self-confidence increases, you will be more comfortable using the authority inherent in your leadership position. Remember, when you have the authority, experience, and education, use them! Don't wait to be asked. Be proud of your strengths and put them to use.

Timing

How much time is there to make the decision? If time is of the essence, you alone may need to make the decision. When emergencies demand quick action, participatory decision making is entirely inappropriate. However, when time is available and others are willing and able to participate, it is often wise to involve them in the process.

Motivation

How motivated are you to make the decision? Would the involvement of others increase your motivation? Are others interested in joining the process? How could you motivate them to become more involved? If you are low on motivation and interest, analyze why. If you readily find all kinds of other activities to keep you busy, ask yourself what purpose your procrastination is serving. Are you uncertain about your abilities, afraid of the outcome, unsure of the risk involved? Think about a decision you have been trying to make—such as changing jobs or careers, losing weight, or ending a relationship. Ask yourself these questions:

1. What would I rather be doing and why?
2. What will others think of me based on my decision?
3. What risk is involved?

4. Do I have all the information I need to make the decision? What
do I lack?

As you answer these questions, remember that your perceptions of the
consequences of your decision may be unrealistic. You may think
massive disapproval will result if you do one thing, yet concrete
information from the world around you indicates that such a catastro-
phe is unlikely.

If you are low on motivation, identify your feelings and resources.
Draw upon the enthusiasm of others and involve them in the decision
to increase your motivation.

Climate

What is the climate surrounding the decision in your work unit? In
the organization? Is it one of trust or suspicion? Do you expect nothing
to result from your decision? What do others involved expect to result
from the decision?

As a leader, you can control the environment of your work unit to
make sure your followers feel comfortable about participating in
making decisions. Introduce them to problem-solving skills, discuss
their role in making decisions, and examine the appropriateness of past
and future decisions with them.

The climate of the organization is primarily determined by others
above you in the hierarchy, but you do have some influence. Look for
opportunities. Initiate discussions with your superiors about the kinds
of decisions that you, your colleagues, and followers are interested in
and able to make. Clarify who is to make which decisions, on which
topics, by which date. It can take a long time to change an unhealthy
climate. Only you can determine how much energy you are willing to
devote to this task. In some organizations, the effort is well worth it; in
others, it may be worth so little that it is best to move on to a healthier
organization.

Group Decision-Making Methods

Two methods are often used in group decision making: voting (either
by majority or plurality) and consensus.

Voting

Most people are familiar with making decisions by vote. In
meetings run according to standard parliamentary procedure, mem-

bers must vote to close discussion on a topic before moving on to the next agenda item. Such a procedure gives every group member an opportunity to become involved.

The voting method is appropriate when there is insufficient time to thoroughly discuss all aspects of an issue. Its effectiveness, however, depends on participants' skills in parliamentary procedures, running meetings, and problem solving. Sometimes members who are more familiar with parliamentary rules can manipulate the vote to meet their needs. Thus there is a chance that a minority may actually get its way. In addition, those who do not get their way will be dissatisfied with the outcome. In other words, though all participants technically have equal power, there are winners and losers in voting.

Consensus

In the consensus method, all group members must agree before a decision is made. When sufficient time is available to discuss an issue thoroughly, consensus is usually preferable to voting, since everyone can come out a winner. In order for consensus to be effective, each participant's ideas must be valued and group members must understand and accept the groundrules. If these are not made clear, some members may rush the process, push for a vote, or otherwise interfere.

Consensus, like voting, utilizes all group members, but to a fuller extent by distributing power more equally among those involved and by relying on each member's satisfaction with the outcome. As a result, the consensus method ensures a higher degree of morale.

Here are some guidelines to follow in using the consensus method:

—Choose a setting where everyone can be comfortable and easily seen and heard. Provide a chalkboard or newsprint pad to record important information.

—Assign a process observer to monitor the group's observance of groundrules.

—Allow enough time for the process to be completed. If the group disbands before consensus is reached, people may lose trust in one another and in the method.

—Avoid arguments. All members should be encouraged to state their opinions and ideas, even if they conflict with others'. Group discussion is fine, but heated arguments can lead people to become defensive and to feel that they, rather than their ideas, are being attacked. If an argument begins to develop, the leader should interrupt and encourage members to paraphrase previous statements before introducing new ideas.

—Be on the alert when people change their position. Make sure position changes result from actual shifts in attitude or opinion, not from a need to "keep the peace."

—Avoid conflict-reducing techniques such as voting and making tradeoffs, which run counter to the purpose of consensus. Instead, ask for a "consensus check," polling everyone's current position on the issue or topic.

Keep these decision-making methods in mind as you learn more about the essential elements of problem solving below.

Steps in Problem Solving

The decision is the outcome or end product. The process by which a decision is reached involves problem solving, which includes six steps:

1. Identifying the problem
2. Analyzing the problem
3. Setting goals and objectives
4. Searching for solutions
5. Planning
6. Evaluating

The time spent on each step depends on the following variables: (1) how much problem analysis is needed, (2) how thoroughly alternative solutions will be analyzed, and (3) how much time is available. Figure 10 illustrates the six steps. Notice that they flow in a cycle; each ending becomes a new beginning. Also note that at any point you may become involved in substeps that necessitate either short or lengthy stops.

As the decision maker, you decide how much time to devote to making the decision, who to involve in the process, and how complex a process to use. Most problems can be categorized into one of three types.

Low. Those that are relatively simple, requiring little time and analysis.

Moderate. Those that are somewhat complex, requiring more time, analysis, and input by others.

Difficult. Those that are highly complex, requiring considerable time to assess, search for solutions, and plan for follow-up activities. Such problems are best solved with the assistance of others who have interest in or experience with the problem.

Problems falling into the low category include decisions about how

Figure 10. The problem-solving cycle.

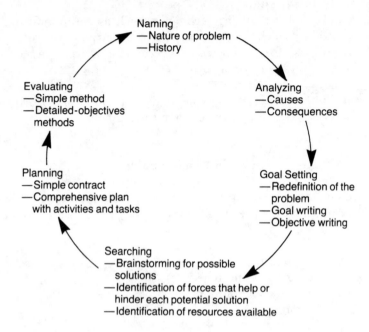

to use your time for a short period, what to eat or wear, which phone call to return. They often carry a low risk for the decision maker, because the consequences are not severe.

For more difficult and complex decisions, there are two problem-solving models: the Compact Problem-Solving Process, for problems in the moderately complex range, especially those of a personal, one-to-one nature; and the Comprehensive Problem-Solving Process, for more difficult problems in groups and organizations, when time is not a pressure and assistance in reaching decisions is available.

The Compact Problem-Solving Process

The Compact Problem-Solving Process runs counter to the norm that individuals should always be strong, self-reliant, and able to solve their problems. With this norm, people are left to deal with their problems alone or are just left alone with their problems. In either case, solutions are frequently never found, slow in coming, or short in duration. The compact model requires that at least two people seek solutions to a problem *collaboratively*. It is based on the assumption that two people can think of more options than one, and can better analyze ideas and develop plans. In addition, it enables the person with a problem to get the emotional support needed to tackle difficult problems.

In the process, each participant generates at least two potentially useful, new solutions to an individual's specific problem. The procedure is completed within 30 minutes. The individuals involved (up to six people works best) must be familiar with all the steps, be committed to a collaborative problem-solving method, agree to abide by the guidelines (outlined below), and make sure they will not be interrupted during the session.

The roles of those in the group include:

The Problem Poser. The person presenting the problem.
The Recorder. The person assigned to do any required writing.
The Timer. The person watching the time and moving the group to the next step when the limit is up. (If only two people are using the method, the last two roles are filled by one person.)

The following description of the steps involved in the process includes the time allotted for each step, questions for participants to answer, and other guidelines. It is important that each step be carried out for the length of time indicated.

Naming the problem

The problem poser takes up to 5 minutes to describe a specific problem to the group. Participants listen carefully, interrupting only when clarification is needed to assist the problem poser in explaining the problem.

The problem poser begins by describing the incident that led to the problem, answering these questions:

Nature of incident
1. Who was involved?
2. What did each person say and do?

History of incident
1. Does this incident have a prior history that makes it particularly problematic? When and where does the problem usually occur?
2. What related experiences in your life set the stage for the incident? What occurred in the other person's life that set the stage for the incident?

Results
1. How did you feel during and after the incident?
2. How do you think the other party felt?
3. What happened just after the incident?

Analyzing the problem and setting goals

The group then spends 5 minutes analyzing the causes of the problem in order to clarify what happened and why. This process gives the problem poser a clearer idea of the outcome she would like.

Down to basics. The problem poser completes each of these sentences in as many ways as she can:
1. "What I really wanted in this situation was. . . ."
2. "What the other person really wanted was. . . ."
3. "The basic conflict is. . . ."

Unique or a pattern. To determine if the problem is part of a pattern, the problem poser responds to these questions:
1. How often has this incident occurred before? Did you and the other person react the same way?
2. Have other people you know experienced the problem?
3. How has the problem been handled in the past? How did it work out?

Goal setting. What do you want to happen?

Searching for solutions

In the next 5 minutes all the members of the group "brainstorm" the problem, each generating as many possible solutions as she or he can. The goal at this point is to generate ideas in quantity, not quality. The recorder writes down all the ideas given by the group, using shorthand if necessary to keep up with people's suggestions. All members follow these groundrules for brainstorming:

Quantity, not quality. Think of as many solutions as possible. The more bizarre, the better.

Piggyback. If someone else's idea triggers a slight variation of some other idea for you, call it out.

No evaluation. All ideas are accepted. No judgments or discussions of pros and cons are allowed at this time.

Time limits. Stop immediately at the end of five minutes.

Planning

In the planning step, the problem poser takes 5 to 7 minutes to evaluate all the ideas suggested and to select those having the greatest potential. The problem poser evaluates each suggestion, using this system:

Impossible: Cross out ideas that are unrealistic or incompatible with your values or situation.

Maybe: Put an M next to those you might consider.

Outstanding: Put an asterisk (*) next to those that strike you as creative, realistic, or appealing.

The group then discusses the most plausible solutions, refining the best ones until they are acceptable to the problem poser. From these, the problem poser chooses a workable solution. This plan is put into writing by the recorder.

Evaluation

The group spends the remaining 8 to 10 minutes reviewing the problem poser's plan and arranging for some method to monitor its progress. Whether the group decides on a series of meetings, lunches, or telephone calls, this follow-up arrangement is essential. Too often, people lose their resolve to try something new in the course of daily routine, or simply slip back into an old behavior pattern. However, if the problem poser commits herself to a plan she believes in and has full support from other members of the group, her chances for success increase drastically. At each follow-up session done in person, the group can review progress and make new suggestions if the problem poser needs to modify the plan. Follow-up should take place fairly soon after the plan is implemented and continue until the problem is resolved.

In summary, the Compact Problem-Solving Process is a collaborative approach that enables the problem poser to take advantage of the goodwill and resources of group members to help her think through a problem. It is a highly flexible process, suited to both personal and professional problems. Group members do not need to be familiar with the details of a personal problem for the approach to be effective.

The Comprehensive Problem-Solving Process

The Comprehensive Problem-Solving Process applies to problems affecting a group of people or the entire organization rather than to an individual's problems. Like the Compact method, it depends on the involvement, cooperation, and knowledge of others.

The process takes 3 to 5 hours and utilizes a series of worksheets. Below is a list of the six steps involved, with the numbers of appropriate worksheets, and the suggested time range for each step. Since a great deal of information will be written on the worksheets, each group will need a "recorder." The time actually devoted to a step will depend on the group's familiarity with the problem and preparation for the session. If members have already talked about a problem, for instance, they will need less time for the "naming the problem" step.

Step	Time
Naming the problem (#28)	20–30 minutes
Analyzing the problem (#29)	10–20 minutes
Setting goals (#30, 31)	35–50 minutes
Searching for solutions (#32, 33, 34)	50–70 minutes
Planning (#35, 36)	40–60 minutes
Evaluating	30–60 minutes

Naming the problem

The group begins by generating statements of the problem—that is, the situation or condition considered to be undesirable. Each person completes the problem statement worksheet (#28), answering the questions and writing a preliminary statement. Members then share their perceptions of the problem. Because initial problem statements often contain more than one problem, clarification is crucial at this point. This step is the foundation of the entire process. Rushing through it will undermine all subsequent steps. If your group discovers it has more than one problem to solve, list all perceived problems and then rank them according to their importance or immediacy. The group can decide then which problem to deal with first, recognizing that other problems can be handled at a later date. A group statement of the problem should be recorded.

Analyzing the problem

The group next explores the causes and consequences of the problem. A cause is what created the problem; a consequence is what is happening or may happen because of the problem.

Each member completes the problem analysis worksheet (#29) to gain further insight into the problem and possible solutions. Responses are discussed until the group reaches a consensus on the causes and consequences. This consensus is recorded.

Setting goals

The third step is divided into two parts: redefinition of the problem and goal setting. By now, the problem—its causes and consequences—should be clearer, and group members should be able

28   NAMING THE PROBLEM: Writing a Problem Statement

Definition: A **problem** is a situation or condition considered to be undesirable.

Time: 20—30 minutes.

Problem assessment:

1. What is the problem?

2. Where is it a problem?

3. When is it a problem?

4. For whom is it a problem?

5. What is likely to happen in the future if something isn't done about the
   problem?

Problem statement:

29   ANALYZING THE PROBLEM: Identifying Causes and Consequences

Definition: A **cause** is what has led to the problem.
                       A **consequence** is what is happening or may happen because of
                       the problem.

Time: 10—20 minutes.

List causes:

1.

2.

3.

4.

5.

6.

Which causes are the most significant?

List consequences:

1.

2.

3.

4.

5.

6.

Which consequences are the most undesirable?

to restate it in more specific terms. Together, the group redefines the undesirable condition or situation using worksheet **#30.** The group must determine how members will benefit by solving the described problem.

After completing the new problem statement, the group focuses on identifying a desirable goal or outcome. Worksheet **#31** provides space for the goal statement and then provides a list of criteria that should be applied to the statement. The statement is reworked until the group agrees on its content and each of the criteria fits.

Searching for solutions

In this step the group thinks of possible solutions to the problem and selects those that are most plausible. The group begins by brainstorming for 10 or 15 minutes, following the guidelines outlined under the Compact Problem-Solving Process. The purpose is to generate a list of potential strategies, or methods for achieving the goal. All the group's ideas are recorded on the strategy worksheet (**#32**). Members then evaluate the list, eliminating approaches that are unrealistic, and assigning an M to those they might consider and an asterisk (*) to those that seem outstanding. After members have chosen two or three of the most promising strategies, they evaluate each one, identifying the helping and hindering forces behind it. Helping forces are those that work in favor of a strategy; hindering forces are those that work against it.

Suppose, for example, that the group's goal is to keep members up to date on their profession. One possible strategy is to hold periodic staff meetings to share the latest techniques and developments in the field. The group may decide that the following forces affect this strategy:

Helping Forces ⟶	⟵ *Hindering Forces*
Most staff members are interested in this idea.	Two staff members are not interested in this idea.
Each staff member reads different professional journals and attends different meetings, so we have the resources available.	We do not have a place to meet where we won't be interrupted. The meetings will take time away from our work.

The group then assesses its influence over the forces identified and determines how to capitalize on the helping forces and minimize the hindering forces. The list of forces and the group's assessment are recorded on the second strategy worksheet (**#33**).

30   GOAL SETTING: Redefining the Problem

Definition: A **problem** is a situation or condition considered to be undesirable.

Time: 10–15 minutes.

Self-interest: Record "what's in it for us" statements about the problem.

Final problem statement: Restate the problem as clearly as possible.

31   GOAL SETTING: Setting a Goal

Definition: A **goal** is a situation or condition considered to be desirable.

Time: 25–35 minutes.

Goal statement:

Target date: _____

Criteria check: Check the goal against these criteria. Is it:

	Yes	No	Maybe
Conceivable—Capable of being put into words?	_____	_____	_____
Achievable—Realistic, given your strengths, abilities, and situation?	_____	_____	_____
Valuable—Acceptable and compatible with your values?	_____	_____	_____
Manageable—Dealing with only one desirable outcome at a time?	_____	_____	_____
Growth-facilitating—Not harmful to you, others, or society?	_____	_____	_____

32   SEARCHING FOR SOLUTIONS: Listing Strategies

Definition: A **strategy** is a method for achieving a goal.

Time: 15–25 minutes.

Strategies	Code
1.	
2.	
3.	
4.	
5.	
6.	
7.	
8.	
9.	
10.	

Definition: A **strategy** is a method for achieving a goal.

Time: 20−25 minutes.

Strategy 1: _____

Helping forces	Hindering forces
1. _____	1. _____
2. _____	2. _____
3. _____	3. _____
4. _____	4. _____

Strategy 2: _____

Helping forces	Hindering forces
1. _____	1. _____
2. _____	2. _____
3. _____	3. _____
4. _____	4. _____

Strategy 3: _____

Helping forces	Hindering forces
1. _____	1. _____
2. _____	2. _____
3. _____	3. _____
4. _____	4. _____

Assessment: Strategy 1   Strategy 2   Strategy 3

1. Which forces can the group influence?

   _____   _____   _____

2. How can the effects of the helping
   forces be increased ?

   _____   _____   _____

3. How can the effects of the hindering
   factors be reduced?

   _____   _____   _____

The group's next task is to analyze the resources available for each strategy. Resources are sources of supply or support. They can be tangible—such as people, money, equipment, and facilities—or intangible—such as time, knowledge, skills, influence or prestige, and energy. The group's analysis is recorded on the third strategy worksheet (#34).

Planning

The group now moves into planning specific activities and tasks to carry out the most important or promising strategy, or perhaps all three. This step of assigning responsibility to members is crucial to the problem-solving effort and requires sincere commitment on the part of the entire group. Assignments will depend on the number of activities involved. If possible, each person should be given responsibility for one major activity and should assist in performing several tasks. Such teamwork is not only necessary but desirable. In addition, the sharing of responsibility gives each member a personal stake in accomplishing the goal.

The group first determines its specific activities—the procedures needed to implement a strategy—and the members responsible for them. This information is listed on the activities worksheet (#35). (One worksheet is used for each strategy to be implemented.) The group then breaks each activity down into different tasks, or work assignments, specifying what will be done, when, by whom, and the resources available. Assignments are recorded on the tasks worksheet (#36).

For instance, in our earlier example, the goal was to provide an update in developments in the profession. A selected strategy was to hold periodic meetings. Some activities could include:

1. Listing areas of concern to the group.
2. Group members identifying areas they will report on.
3. Inviting outside resource people to do presentations.

For activity #3, a task worksheet might read:

	Task	By when?	By whom?	Resources
1.	Chairperson chosen to head committee	March 1	Group decides	
2.	List areas of concern not covered by group members' reports	March 8	Chairperson	Group members
3.	Obtain suggestions for presenters	March 15	Chairperson	Professional journals
4.	Contact and schedule selected presenters	March 30	Chairperson	

Evaluating

In the final step, the group assesses the entire process. If others in the group have temporarily assumed leadership roles during the meeting, you as designated leader must now reassume charge. Your responsibility is to summarize the process, restating the problem, goal, strategies, and major activities. You might also ask the group to evaluate the method itself, raising some of these questions:

1. How did you feel before, during, and after using this method?
2. What was the most useful part? The least useful?
3. What would have made the process more constructive? Room we used? Amount of time?
4. How can we use this process in the future? When should we do it again?
5. What changes need to be made?

As leader, you are also responsible for monitoring the plan. Be sure that a final problem, goal, and strategy statement is prepared. Collect the activities and tasks worksheets, review them, and distribute final copies so that every participant knows her or his part in the plan. This will reduce misunderstandings and improve accountability—both of which are crucial to success.

Use a Gantt chart (**#37**) to monitor the progress of each activity. Describe the activity at the top of the chart and list the tasks involved down the left-hand column. Write the name or initials of the person assigned to each task in the "Who" column. The "Dates" columns cover a period of one month. Opposite each task, draw a horizontal line from the date the task is to be started to the date that it is scheduled to be completed.

Give a copy of the chart to all participants so they will understand how their particular tasks fit into the whole plan. As tasks are completed, make a slash (/) on the line below that date. If more time is needed, extend the solid line with a dotted line to show the new deadline. Keep the chart handy for periodic review.

A Positive Approach to Decision Making

Making appropriate decisions is the backbone of effective leadership. In addition to problem-solving skills, leaders must have a positive approach to decision making.

Assess your attitude. Your attitude toward making decisions affects

34   SEARCHING FOR SOLUTIONS: Looking at Resources

Definition: A *resource* is a source of supply or support.

Time: 15–20 minutes.

Strategy: 1. _____

2. _____

3. _____

Resource	Is the resource needed for this strategy?			Is the resource available?			If not available, can the resource be obtained?		
	1	2	3	1	2	3	1	2	3
Personnel									
Money									
Equipment									
Facilities									
Time									
Knowledge									
Skill									
Influence or prestige									
Energy									

35   PLANNING: Selecting Activities

Definition: An **activity** is a specific procedure for implementing a strategy.

Time: 20—30 minutes.

Strategy: _____

Activities	Person responsible
1.	
2.	
3.	
4.	
5.	
6.	
7.	
8.	
9.	
10.	

Definition: A **task** is a specific work assignment, usually with a deadline.

Time: 20–25 minutes.

Strategy: _____

Activity: _____

Tasks	By when?	By whom?	Resources?
1.			
2.			
3.			
4.			
5.			
6.			
7.			
8.			
9.			
10.			

37 GENERAL-PURPOSE GANTT CHART

Activity:

Date:

Tasks	Who	Dates

the kinds of decisions you make. As a leader, you should look at decision making as an opportunity to unleash your creative powers, to grow, to utilize the resources of those around you, and to effect change in your organization and in society. Examine your attitudes. Are you open to growth? Do you look upon decision making as a risk or an opportunity?

Keep an open mind. Decision making is a creative process that needs nurturing—to allow ideas to emerge, gestate, be studied and weighed. It requires an openness to the novel or unusual and a willingness to withhold judgment until all options have emerged. Although the process is hard work, it is also rewarding.

Trust yourself. Making decisions takes courage—the courage to risk others' disapproval and to be different or ahead of your time. Trust your own intelligence, feelings, and judgments. Act on your experience and good sense.

Learn from your mistakes. A decision maker must be willing to accept her limits, to recognize that she, like other mortals, will at times make poor and inappropriate decisions. Yet an effective leader does not lament, "How dumb I was to make that decision!" Instead, she says, "Well, I made the best decision I could *at that time*"—and believes that statement. Both women and men tend to judge themselves harshly and to have great difficulty accepting their mistakes. It is important to realize and *believe* that you functioned in the best way you could at the time. If the results were not favorable, ask yourself: "What did I learn?" You learn by doing, by testing your limits, and by applying what you learned to new situations. Expect to make some inappropriate decisions and learn to build with the rocks you stumble over.

RESOURCES

Bowers, David G. *Systems of Organization*. Ann Arbor: University of Michigan Press, 1976.

Davis, Larry Nolan, and Earl McCallon. *Planning, Conducting, and Evaluating Workshops*. Austin, TX: Learning Concepts, 1974.

Jones, Garfield. *Parliamentary Procedure at a Glance*. New York: Hawthorne Books, 1971.

Lippitt, Ronald, Jean Watson, and Bruce Westley. *The Dynamics of Planned Change*. New York: Harcourt, Brace, 1958.

"Nuclear Problem-Solving Process," in *A Primer for Social Literacy Training: Liberating Approaches to Discipline Problems*. Distributed by the Social Literacy Project, 459 Hills South, University of Massachusetts, Amherst, MA 01002.

Schmuch, Richard, et al. *Handbook of Organizational Development in Schools*. Palo Alto, CA: Mayfield Publishing, 1972.

Scholz, Nelle, Judith Prince and Gordon Miller. *How to Decide: A Guide for Women*. New York: College Entrance Examination Board, 1975.

Thornton, Leslie J. *Problem Solving*. Ann Arbor: University of Michigan, 1977.

9

Planning for change

IT HAS BEEN SAID that there are three kinds of people: those who make things happen, those who watch things happen, and those who wonder what happened. Because the planning function is essential to effective organizational leadership, leaders cannot watch or wonder; they must do and plan. An organization without a top-level leader skilled in planning is like a ship without a captain to determine its course. An organization without middle- and lower-level leaders skilled in implementing plans is like a ship without lieutenants to lead the crew.

As observed in previous chapters, women are sometimes at a disadvantage in leadership positions because they have not developed long-term planning skills. In setting personal goals, they tend to focus on short-term job planning rather than on long-term career planning. On the job, they tend to be more comfortable with day-to-day, operational planning than with long-range, strategic planning. These patterns have important implications for women in or entering middle and top management, where long-term planning is essential. This chapter examines ways to deal with the problem and suggests an approach to building planning skills.

Planning in the Organization

Leaders at different levels of the organization participate in different types of planning, and to different degrees, as illustrated in Figure 11. The solid triangle represents the hierarchy of an organization, with the executive and top managers at the top and the low-level supervisors at

Figure 11. The planning function.

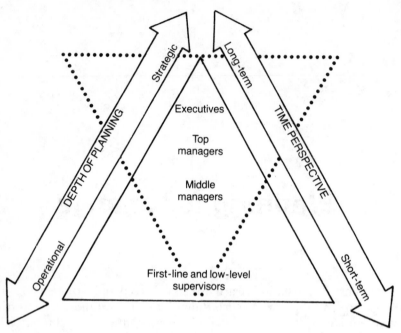

the bottom. The dotted triangle represents the involvement of the individuals, by level, in the planning process. The small number of managers at the top engage in the majority of the planning activities and the large number at the bottom engage in very few planning activities. The arrows represent the time and depth aspects of planning: The leaders at the top engage in strategic, long-term planning, whereas supervisors engage in operational, short-term planning.

As shown in chart **#38,** the planning process entails nine basic skills or operations: forecasting, setting objectives, developing strategies, analyzing risks, creating programs, assigning responsibility, budgeting resources, scheduling and standardizing activities, and controlling and monitoring the plan. These nine elements are grouped according to level of leadership below:

The creators: Planning at the top

Imagine yourself on top of the tallest skyscraper in your city. Without the usual obstructions—buildings, trees, cars—you can see in all directions for great distances. Now imagine yourself sitting in the

38 PLANNING SKILLS

	First-line/Low	Middle	Top	Executive
Forecasting		• Identifies organizational problems		• Assesses economic, social, and political factors related to organization's needs • Determines organizational direction and goals
Setting objectives	• Sets short-term objectives	• Determines intermediate objectives within long-term goals	• Interprets policy • Determines long-term objectives	• Determines policy
Developing strategies			• Identifies alternative strategies	• Approves recommended strategies
Analyzing risks		• Analyzes risk potential for existing organizational procedures	• Weighs gains and losses for proposed strategies	• Analyzes risk to organization's goals and policies
Creating programs		• Organizes short-term programs		• Establishes policy to support programs
Assigning responsibilities	• Assigns work according to established goals and objectives			
Budgeting resources	• Operates within stated resource limitations	• Develops budget and human resource needs	• Recommends budgets • Allocates human resources	• Approves budget
Scheduling and standardizing	• Establishes operational procedures for work units • Schedules work	• Establishes organizational procedures to implement policy		
Controlling and monitoring	• Complies with established procedures	• Assesses effectiveness of operational procedures • Recommends changes	• Evaluates policies, objectives, and procedures • Recommends changes	• Continually assesses organizational and environmental factors • Approves recommendations

Leadership Level	Elements of Planning
Creators	
Executives	Forecasting
Top managers	Setting objectives
	Developing strategies
	Analyzing risks
Translators	
Middle managers	Creating programs
	Assigning responsibility
	Budgeting resources
Implementors	
Low-level managers	Scheduling and standardizing activities
First-line supervisors	Controlling and monitoring

chair of the current head of your organization. This person "sees" numerous people, tangible assets, economic indicators, social trends, and potential markets for the product or service provided by the organization. In other words, the executive's picture from her or his chair is similar to your picture from the skyscraper: the Gestalt, or the whole, is perceived.

The planner at the top is a visionary who looks beyond day-to-day operations to broader, long-term goals. Using both conceptual and cognitive skills, the planner proactively initiates ideas and watches for potential problems. The top-level planner is persistently curious, questioning, and probing. She or he is the "advance scout" on the organization's journey into the future.

Planners at the top are the creators. Their plans affect both daily operational programs and procedures and the organization's future direction. The top-level planner is skilled in forecasting, setting objectives, developing strategies, and analyzing risks. In forecasting, the planner makes a careful analysis of the economic, social, and political forces at work in society and in the organization. On the basis of this analysis, the top manager determines long-term objectives and develops appropriate strategies to achieve them, taking into account the potential gains and losses of each proposed strategy. In this determination, the planner must weigh actual results against organizational goals, immediate needs against future demands, and desirable ends against available means.

Thus planners at the top utilize imagination, analytical skills, instinct, and judgment. They adopt a positive attitude toward taking risks and seek ways to build the future from the present. Their goal is to rid the organization of unproductive and obsolete policies, programs, and procedures and to create productive ones that reflect its ongoing needs.

The translators: Middle managers

Middle managers, as translators, are responsible for moving from the conceptual to the operational. Their task is to convert the long-term plans developed by top management into programs of action, identifying specific steps needed to accomplish objectives, assigning responsibilities to certain employees, and determining budget requirements. At this level, knowledge of the total organization is essential.

Middle managers must deal with abstractions and ambiguities, determine priorities amid conflicting objectives, work with tendencies and probabilities rather than certainties, and discern correlations as well as cause-and-effect relationships. Middle managers participate with top management in assessing the effectiveness of policies and procedures, recommend changes, organize programs, allocate human and fiscal resources, and establish procedures that reflect organizational policies.

The implementors: Planning at the lower levels

First-line supervisors and low-level managers are the implementors. They focus on daily operational procedures, supervision, and monitoring and recommend changes to their bosses. Because they operate from a short-term perspective, they rarely engage in strategic, conceptual planning. Leaders at this level need technical expertise and familiarity with established organizational procedures, rules, and regulations. They are responsible for scheduling activities to accomplish specific short-term objectives, setting standards for planned activities, and developing methods to monitor the progress of these operations.

Assessing Your Planning Skills

You are now ready to assess your planning skills. As before, decide whether you want to focus on skills in your current or target leadership position. Review chart **#38** to determine the skills you already possess. Rate these strengths with the following code:

+3   Highly developed
+2   Somewhat developed
+1   Minimally developed

For instance, if you have had limited experience in setting short-term objectives, you might rate yourself +1.

Next, review the chart to identify the skills you'd like to develop more fully. Use a similar rating system:

        - 1   Needs minimal development
        - 2   Needs some development
        - 3   Needs considerable development

For instance, if you have had little opportunity to determine long-term objectives, you might rate yourself as − 2.

List each of the skills you'd like to develop on the planning sheet in chart #39, in the order in which you'd like to develop them.

This chapter examines several strategies for developing planning skills, such as looking at your philosophy (including your psychological attitudes), enhancing your intellectual development, and gaining experience. All of these will help you to more effectively use the planning skills listed on chart #38. Additional planning skills are covered in other parts of this book. For example, setting objectives, assigning responsibilities, and scheduling employees' work are discussed in Chapter 8; analyzing risk is discussed in Chapter 10. And, of course, there are additional topics found in the resources section at the end of each chapter.

Evaluating Your Philosophy

In preparing for planning responsibilities, it is extremely important to be clear on your own philosophy—your beliefs and attitudes about yourself and others, your view of human nature, and your conception of the role of institutions in society. Your beliefs about yourself carry over into your relationships with others. High regard for yourself leads you to respect others as well. Conversely, a poor self-concept can lead you to distrust others. (Suggestions for improving your self-concept are given in Chapter 10.)

Each decision a leader makes reflects either a personal or organizational philosophy. If, for instance, you believe that people are inherently good and capable of making wise decisions for their own lives, then the decisions you make and any short- or long-term plans you set will reflect this philosophy. It is also important to determine whether your behavior actually reflects your philosophy. Do you act on your beliefs? For example, if you believe that people should be encouraged to move from dependence to independence, you might ask yourself if you encourage your followers to try new activities and if you take such risks yourself?

The woman leader, whether implementor, translator, or creator, continually tests her philosophy as demands are placed on her to adapt to the goals, policies, norms, and procedures of the organization. In most organizations, for example, advancement is given to those who

39 PLANNING SHEET FOR SKILLS IN PLANNING

Skills I want to develop	Order of development	Found in chapter	Additional resources

adhere to established norms. These include certain expectations about dress, the expression or denial of emotions, competition, and willingness to devote long hours to work. Because norms for the working world have been developed and perpetuated by men, women are expected to "become like men" and accept these norms for themselves in order to succeed. The adoption of these norms as the standards against which others are judged leads organizations to ask why women do not perform as well as men for the organization *rather* than why the organization does not perform as well for women as it does for men. By viewing women rather than itself as the problem, the organization seeks ways to change women to bring them "up" to its standards. By focusing on the "victim" of sexism, the organization never questions the validity or justice of "gendo-centric" standards. The pervasiveness of this approach demands that women be clear about their philosophies and firm in their belief in themselves.

Making the Psychological Shift

Only *you* can decide if you really want to move into increasingly responsible leadership positions. If you do, you will also need to make a psychological shift. For example, the specific, day-to-day operational aspects of planning are the responsibility of lower-level leaders and should not be carried over into higher levels, where the focus is on broad, long-term planning responsibilities. As you advance in the organization, you will have to give up familiar and comfortable activities that you do well, expand your horizons, and take risks in new job functions. This shift in focus is crucial to effective leadership at higher levels.

This crucial shift is not only essential but possible. Women have had innumerable experiences in planning, usually in unpaid community or domestic responsibilities. These can be the foundation for applying planning techniques to a work setting.

Expanding Your Intellectual Abilities

How does women's intelligence measure up to men's? Maccoby[1] found that from early childhood, males appear to be superior to females in spatial and analytic ability, and that females appear to be superior in verbal ability. Montagu reviewed the scientific findings on the intellectual functions of both sexes and concluded that "with the exception of the tests for arithmetic, mathematics, mechanics, and mazes, females achieve significantly and consistently higher scores on the intelligence tests than males."[2] Using intelligence tests as a measure, he found no evidence to suggest that the female is intellectually inferior to the male.

Thus, theoretically, women leaders responsible for conceptual and cognitive planning should be able to handle this task as well as men. This is not necessarily the case. Intelligence is very closely related to cultural experience. In other words, how a person develops her or his intellectual potential will depend on the environment. Female children and adolescents are given less encouragement than their male counterparts to develop the ability to think analytically and abstractly. It is this difference in socialization that puts women at a disadvantage in planning tasks.

Women do learn analytical skills, but they have been taught to focus on analyzing people and relationships, not things and data. Moreover, many women fail to recognize that they have developed and applied strategic planning in their personal lives and in their political and community involvements. Recognizing the impact of your schooling and socialization on leadership potential is the first step. Committing yourself to building on the intellectual abilities and strategic planning skills you already possess is the next.

What messages have you received in the past about your intellectual abilities? Are you a woman who was not encouraged or given the opportunity to develop conceptual skills? Are you a woman who was encouraged until you reached puberty—or until you were of a "marriageable" age? How do these messages affect your perceptions of your intelligence?

If you have little confidence in your abilities, take action. Read books, enroll in continuing-education programs, and attend workshops that will stimulate your thinking. Take courses in philosophy, logic, mathematics, social movements, planning, and futuristics. The many messages you've internalized may tell you that you can't understand analytical or conceptual problems. But keep in mind that those messages were intended to prepare you for the homemaking role—one that is increasingly less functional in today's society. Women today are expanding their roles and more fully participating in work outside the home. As a result, your internal "tapes" may be out of date and in need of revision.

Gaining Experience in Planning

As a final step in preparing for planning responsibilities, you should obtain as much experience as you can in planning, especially long-term and broad-perspective planning.

Become an astute observer. Assume the perspective of those responsible for long-term planning. Look at the organization through their eyes; imagine what they are observing, what they are thinking. Isolate potential problems and trends by putting together bits and pieces of information.

Assist a planner. Look for opportunities to work with someone who is responsible for developing a plan. Analyze the process and observe which of the nine planning operations are involved. Assist in carrying out parts of the plan. Most important, learn from the other person's experience as a planner.

Seek help from a mentor. Mentors can directly assist you in developing planning skills. Read the section on mentors in Chapter 10. Ask your mentor for suggestions on how to develop planning skills.

Look above you. Inquire about positions in the organization that involve planning. Learn on the job if necessary, but be willing to tackle leadership positions that utilize conceptual, long-range planning skills.

Plan your life with a long-term perspective. The goal of this book is to help you prepare for a long-term career in leadership. In setting your preliminary career goal and using the assessment tools throughout the book, you have in fact been planning your own life. With your career goal in mind and an idea of your strengths and weaknesses, you are ready to make it happen. Read on.

REFERENCES

1. Eleanor E. Maccoby, "Sex Differences in Intellectual Functioning," in *Development of Sex Differences,* E. Maccoby, ed. (Stanford, CA: Stanford University Press, 1966), pp. 25–55.
2. Ashley Montagu, *The Natural Superiority of Women* (New York: Collier Books, 1972), p. 124.

RESOURCES

Churchman, C. West. *The Systems Approach.* New York: Dell, 1968.

Drucker, Peter F. *Managing for Results.* New York: Harper & Row, 1964.

Drucker, Peter F. *Management: Tasks, Responsibilities, Practices.* New York: Harper & Row, 1974.

Katz, R. L. "Skills of An Effective Administrator." *Harvard Business Review,* September–October 1974, pp. 90–108.

Levin, Richard, and Charles Kirkpatrick. *Planning and Control with PERT/CPM.* New York: McGraw-Hill, 1966.

Livingston, J. S. "Myth of the Well-Educated Manager." *Harvard Business Review,* January–February 1971, pp. 79–89.

Mann, F. C. "Toward an Understanding of the Leadership Role in Formal

Organization," in Dubin, Homans, and Miller, eds., *Leadership and Productivity*. San Francisco: Chandler Publishing Company, 1965.

Morgan, John. *Managing Change*. New York: McGraw-Hill, 1972.

Pfiffner, J. M., and F. P. Sherwood. *Administrative Organization*. Englewood Cliffs, NJ: Prentice-Hall, 1960.

10

Making it happen

No ONE can afford to merely let things happen. If you seek success, you will have to make things happen. You have completed the first stages of your journey to effective leadership by clarifying your goals, strengths, and needs; by reflecting on and writing about your feelings and thoughts; and by applying some of the results. You are now ready for the final stage, in which you organize the information you have gathered—about yourself, leadership, and organizations—into a plan of action.

Before you can develop a plan, you must review your lifetime career goal and leadership skills. Next, assess the personal and environmental variables that can either enhance or limit your chances of success. These include your self-concept, your risk-taking style, and your resources (time, money, health, people, and organizations). Although some of these variables may currently be blocks to your success, each can be changed to a booster. The final step is to develop a formal plan for achieving your goal.

Your Career Goal and Leadership Skills

Your road to effective leadership has probably taken many turns, with some delays and setbacks, but also with some progress. You began the journey with a preliminary assessment of your lifetime goals and your leadership skills, and it is now time to review.

Return to Chapter 1, where you wrote your initial career goal, specifying the leadership position you wanted in five years, the activities

40	LEADERSHIP STRENGTHS AND NEEDS	
Leadership dimension	Strengths	Areas to develop
Communication		
Human relations		
Supervision		
Counseling		
Management science		
Decision making		
Planning		

involved, the kind of profession, and the geographic location. How accurately does this statement reflect your direction now that you've completed the book? If there are modifications, rewrite the goal to reflect those changes.

Next, review your strengths and needs for leadership skills by examining the skill charts and planning sheets at the beginning of Chapters 3–9. You are now ready to summarize what you know and what you need to learn. On chart #40, list all your strengths—what you already possess in skills, aptitudes, attitudes, and behaviors—and your needs—skills that you want to learn, extend, or reinforce.

Improving Your Self-Concept

When the winner of a high-jumping contest was asked how she knew she would win, she replied, "When you like yourself, you just spring forward!" In other words, what you think of yourself affects your ability to leap. What do you think of yourself and how does this affect your abilities to be a leader?

On the self-concept continuum below, rate your general attitude toward yourself, placing an X in the space that most closely matches your self-evaluation. Try not to let your present state of mind color your assessment—for example, if you are especially discouraged or have just had a marvelous success. Focus on how you generally feel about yourself.

/ _____/ _____/ _____/ _____/ _____/ _____/

| I love myself | I like myself a lot but see a few weak- nesses | I see more strengths than weak- nesses | I see an equal num- ber of strengths and weak- nesses | I dislike myself a lot and see few strengths | I hate myself |

The way you view yourself affects how you view the world and how you behave. Sara, for example, does not trust herself to make a decision; she doubts her intellectual ability to analyze a problem, sort out alternatives, and select the most appropriate solution. Because of her self-image, she considers others, especially men, to be more skilled in making decisions and thus defers to them. As a result, others often question her abilities and assume responsibility for making her deci- sions, ignoring her as a resource.

Barbara, on the other hand, has worked to change her negative self-concept. Previously, she felt powerless and believed that things happened *to* her. Over time, she came to recognize the tremendous power she had over the direction of her life and her ability to make things happen *for* her. As a result, she has actively determined the leadership role she wants and has taken the risk of leaving her teaching job to obtain her master's in business administration (MBA). Other people's attitudes toward her have changed, and she is seen as a powerful and determined woman.

Assess the positive and negative views you have of yourself. Ask yourself: "What do I believe about my intellectual, spiritual, physical, and emotional self?" Write your responses in the appropriate places in chart #41. For example:

Intellectual: "I feel rather dumb." or "I don't know everything, but can always learn."

Spiritual: "I feel alone." or "I feel part of a larger system."

Physical: "I don't have the stamina to jog." or "I may be over 30, but I can jog at my own pace."

Emotional: "I am too emotional." or "Expressing my feelings is healthy."

As you read your responses, add up how many negative and positive beliefs you hold about yourself. Are you surprised? Why or

41   SELF-ASSESSMENT WORKSHEET

A. Intellectual self

    1. _____

    2. _____

    3. _____

B. Spiritual self

    1. _____

    2. _____

    3. _____

C. Physical self

    1. _____

    2. _____

    3. _____

D. Emotional self

    1. _____

    2. _____

    3. _____

Total positive responses _____

  Responses important for leadership _____

Total negative responses _____

  Responses hindering development in leadership _____

why not? Which of your positive beliefs are important for leadership? How can you strengthen these beliefs? Which of your negative beliefs are barriers to your development as a leader? Which are more easily changed? Which are more difficult and persistent?

A positive self-concept is a crucial aspect of leadership. The exercises below are designed to help you reinforce your positive views about yourself. Read them through first to see which ones best fit your needs.

Exercise 1: An already successful me

For this exercise, you must be alone in a quiet place for 15 to 30 minutes. You can do it as you lie in bed in the morning or evening or as you sit at work or at home. Either close your eyes or face a blank wall. Imagine that a movie is about to start and that you are the main character. Every scene pictures you as successful. Create the details around you. If you were successful and loved and believed in yourself, what would be happening? Where would you be? What would you be doing? Who would be around you? How would you react to them and they to you? How would your body look and feel?

Run this movie in your head for at least 15 minutes. Let your imagination flow. Change the scenes, add new people, places, and events—but in each case picture yourself as confident and successful. Repeat the exercise every day for at least two weeks. You may want to record some of your thoughts following each movie to see if they affect your daily activities. Viewing yourself as successful at least once a day sets the stage for it to happen.

Exercise 2: The picture of success

Go through several magazines and cut out pictures of women who are successful or represent a successful image to you. Buy a piece of poster paper, at least 2' × 3' in size, and put a recent picture of you in the middle. Paste the pictures of these successful women around you. Give your collage a self-affirming title, such as "A Picture of Success," "The Successful Ones," or "Onward and Upward." Post it where you will see it often. Study it. Admire it. Show it to others.

Exercise 3: IALAC, or I am loveable and capable[1]

Write down the many ways in which you are a loving and capable person. Try to list at least ten different ways, but don't be concerned if you cannot do so at this time. Many women find it difficult to complete such a list. Yet if they were asked to write ten ways they weren't loving and capable, they would probably have little problem. The purpose of this exercise is to help you reverse the tendency to focus on your negative aspects by emphasizing your positive sides.

Next, ask others you trust to tell you ways in which they see you as loveable and capable. If any response they give is not on your list, add it; if it is on the list, put a check mark next to the item to indicate that someone besides you sees that characteristic.

When your list is complete, copy it on an index card. Post it on your mirror, lay it on your desk, or carry it with you. In other words, keep it visible and handy—and look at it regularly. Memorize the items until you can quickly name them all. As you become aware of new traits, add them to your list. Use the card for periodic "reality checks," especially during low periods.

Exercise 4: My successes in life

This exercise, like some of those previously suggested, helps you focus on aspects about yourself that are too often forgotten or glossed over. Recording your successes in life can help build your sense of self-worth. They need not be major accomplishments. For instance, one friend recalls how successful she felt as a child when she was able to "burp" a Tupperware lid!

On chart **#42,** list your successes from particular periods, as outlined on the left. Review these successes and fill in the remaining columns. What type of success was it—intellectual, spiritual, emotional, or physical? A combination? Who perceived it as a success? You? Who else? Examine your completed list. What types of successes do you generally have? Is there variety or homogeneity? Who recognized your successes?

Women tend to rely on others for validation of their successes. Such dependence often limits their activities to those approved by others. Do you want to limit yourself in that way? If not, monitor your activities from this day on. For each one, ask yourself: "Will I be proud of doing this?" "Does it reflect what is important to me and my self-worth?" If your answer is yes, you can do it and feel successful—even if no one else recognizes it. If it meets your needs, you are successful. If you ask yourself, "What will others think if I do this?" also ask if their recognition is the sole criterion for what is successful to you.

Past successes are the foundation for future successes. Successful people do not "start from scratch" when they move into new projects or activities; they build on what they already know, the skills they already have, and the accomplishments they have accumulated. As you face a challenge, reflect on what was successful for you in the past and draw from this strength. If you are assigned to a department that is in need

42   SUCCESS RECORD

Age	Successes	Type	Recognized by
Early childhood (1–6)			
Middle childhood (7–12)			
Young adulthood (13–19)			
Twenties			
Thirties			
Forties			
Fifties			
Sixties			

of reorganization, keep in mind that even though the situation is new, your organizing skills are not. Giving yourself credit for what you know builds your confidence and thus your ability to succeed in new endeavors.

Exercise 5: My body speaks

Did you know that 90 percent of all messages are conveyed by the body? A positive or negative self-concept is reflected in the way you carry and use your body. Look at yourself and evaluate what your body says about how you feel about yourself. Monitor your nonverbal messages.

Posture: How do you stand and sit? With your body erect, shoulders back, arms relaxed?

Voice: How is your message conveyed? Is your tone clear, steady, uncertain, high- or low-pitched?

Facial expression: What is your facial expression? Does it show attentiveness or disinterest? How much eye contact do you use? Do you smile frequently or infrequently? Appropriately or inappropriately?

Health: What is the physical condition of your body? Is your weight appropriate for your size and age? Are there signs of overuse of any drugs, tobacco, or alcohol?

Handshake: Is your handshake strong or limp? Do you extend your hand or wait for someone else to make the first move?

To improve your self-concept, take charge of your life:

—Walk and sit straight—even if you don't always feel confident!
—Talk clearly and assuredly—even if you aren't so sure of yourself!
—Look alert and attentive—even if your mind is elsewhere!
—Lose weight, stop using drugs to cope, start exercising regularly—even if you've done the opposite all your life!
—Reach out and shake hands firmly—even before the other person!

Move, talk, and act confidently and you'll feel that way.

Improving Your Risk-Taking Skill

A turtle moves ahead only by sticking out its neck.

Risks are a part of daily existence. Look at some common risks you take every day:

Taking a shower in a bathtub.
Deciding what you will wear.
Driving your car to work.
Eating certain foods or eating too much.
Speaking out with your own ideas.
Correcting someone's sexist or racist behavior.

What is a risk? It is a change from the ordinary, the routine, the safe. It is moving forward from one spot to another, from one idea to another, from one value to another, from one behavior to another.

How do women view risk?

The continuum below represents two diverse views of risk taking. At the far left is Annie Avoider, who fears crossing the street, rarely goes out of her house, and wears only clothes that someone else suggests to her. At the right is Tammie Taker, who plunges into all risks, never looking right or left. She crosses the street wherever she wants, marches into any group and takes over immediately, and wears whatever she feels like. Write "Me" at the point on the continuum that represents you most of the time.

/ _____/ _____/ _____/ _____/ _____/
Annie   Tammie
Avoider   Taker

Now place an X where you'd like to be and draw a line between the two points. For instance, if you feel you are somewhat reluctant to take risks but would like to take more, your line might look like this:

                Me ————————————————————————————▶ X
/ _____/ _____/ _____/ _____/
Annie   Tammie
Avoider   Taker

If you see yourself as taking too many risks without enough consideration for the situation, your continuum might look like this:

```
                                    X ◄──────── Me
/ _____/ _____/ _____/ _____/ _____/
Annie                                              Tammie
Avoider                                            Taker
```

In their study of 100 women in management, Hennig and Jardim found that women differed significantly from their male colleagues in their views on taking risks.[2] Women viewed risk very narrowly: it brought loss, danger, injury, ruin, or hurt. Men, on the other hand, saw risk more broadly: it carried potential for both opportunity and danger, gain and setback, win and loss. In other words, women had learned to view risk taking negatively, while men had learned to weigh its potential for negative and positive results.

Women and men also differed in their perspective on the consequences of risk. Women looked at how the risk would affect their immediate situation. Men looked at risk in terms of the future: at how the risk would affect their career, their ability to fulfill their goals, and their opportunities.

Risk and leadership

It is important for women to develop a more positive approach to risk. Achieving your goals, both lifetime and immediate, requires taking risks. To make things happen in your life, you must take risks. Leadership also involves risk, and to be effective, you must enhance your ability to take risks rationally and appropriately. What are some common risks that you as a leader might face?

—Asserting yourself and asking for necessary resources in order to carry out a project.
—Revealing your vulnerabilities to those who supervise you and to those you lead.
—Giving negative feedback to those you supervise.
—Confronting conflict with others or between members of the group.
—Not taking any risks.
—Making decisions.
—Being a leader of men.
—Working in a setting where women are in the minority.

Clearly, to be an effective leader you need a positive attitude toward risks that allows you to learn from them. To build such an attitude, you must:

—Ask yourself what you might gain—as well as lose—by taking a risk.
—Determine how the risk might affect your long-term personal and professional goals.
—Become fully aware of the environment in which you are taking the risks and remove any "blinders."
—Increase the number of moderate-level risks you take.
—Develop confidence in your ability to deal with the results and learn from the experience.

What risks will you take?

Risks can be categorized into high, moderate, and low. The level at which you view a risk depends on you; what is high risk for one person may be moderate or low for another. For instance, Jean becomes immobilized when she is asked to present her opinion in a meeting. The risk for her is so high that she dreads attending the meeting, loses sleep, stumbles over her words, and leaves out many of the ideas she wanted to present. Carrie, on the other hand, views the same situation as a low risk; she is confident when called upon, speaks clearly, and presents her thoughts coherently.

Imagine that you are sitting informally with several people at work, including subordinates, your boss, and your peers. You are asked to share certain information with them, as outlined on chart **#43.** As you read each statement, decide if you would disclose that information to your subordinates, boss, or peers. In the appropriate columns, write "yes" if you would freely reveal the information, "maybe" if you might, and "no" if you wouldn't under any circumstances.

This exercise can help you determine what you are willing to reveal to people at work, the value you place on certain items of information about yourself, and the situations in which you are willing to disclose information. If you repeated the exercise with different people (loved ones, close friends, parents, children, acquaintances, or complete strangers), your willingness to disclose information might change considerably.

Men and women differ in the types of information they are willing to disclose. Men often have a difficult time sharing doubts, problems they are having with a spouse or loved one, or information that might reveal their vulnerabilities. To disclose such information, they must

43   INFORMATION SHARING

Information	Tell subordi- nates	Tell boss	Tell peers
1. Tell something that happened today that pleased you.	_____	_____	_____
2. Take something from your purse or wallet and comment on it.	_____	_____	_____
3. Relate an embarrassing moment.	_____	_____	_____
4. Tell about a time when you were very angry with a man at work and what happened.	_____	_____	_____
5. Give negative feedback to each person in the group.	_____	_____	_____
6. Tell five things that you really like about yourself.	_____	_____	_____
7. Tell about your lifetime goals.	_____	_____	_____
8. Share a sexual fantasy.	_____	_____	_____
9. Ask for negative feedback about yourself.	_____	_____	_____

work against the message they have learned from childhood—that men must be strong at all times. Women often have a difficult time revealing information that might lead others to criticize them. They must work against patterns that have taught them to depend on other people's approval.

These differences between men and women can create problems at work unless they are recognized and accepted without judging one pattern as superior. This does not mean that people should feel free to disclose all information to everyone. To do so could be suicidal. However, women need to learn to unlock their dependence on approval so that they can reveal more of their ideas and opinions. Men need to overcome their fear of showing weakness so they can share their more sensitive feelings with others.

Be smart in taking risks

When you are preparing to take a risk, you must assess not only what you are willing to risk but also the situation or environment in which you are taking it. Tammie Taker has not considered the important elements of her environment if, for example, she wears whatever she wants to work. Her organization, like most others, has norms on dress, and judgments about her are influenced by her choice of clothing. The risk is high if others react so strongly to her dress that they do not see beyond to who she really is and what she has to contribute. Because she has not taken her environment into account, she has unnecessarily increased the level of the risk.

Therefore, systematically study your environment. Think about it as if you were planning a military strategy. You need to know your strengths, your available resources, the variables against you (what the "enemy" has to counter your attack), and any other factors (the weather, your psychological readiness, and so on). Once you have studied your environment and know exactly what is involved, you will have a clearer idea about risks involved.

Approaches to taking risks

Identifying your personal approach to taking risks is the first step in understanding and improving your abilities in this area. How do you perceive risk? What risks have you taken that are low, moderate, and high? The risk chart (#44) helps you answer these questions. Recall three risks you have taken in both your personal and professional life and fill in the information on the chart. Then review what you have recorded and ask yourself the following questions:

1. How often do I take risks? Do I take more low, moderate, or high risks?
2. How do the risks differ at each level? How do they differ between work and personal?
3. What are my feelings before, during, and after taking risks? Am I afraid of taking a high risk and relieved when it is over?
4. Looking back, did the risks I took have opportunities for both loss *and* gain?
5. How many options did I consider as I determined my tactics? How did I determine my options? If I didn't consider many options, why not?

44   RISK CHART

	What was the risk?	What were my feelings before, during, and after taking the risk?	What did I gain?	What did I lose?	What options did I consider? What else should I have considered?
High risk Work					
Personal					
Moderate risk Work					
Personal					
Low risk Work					
Personal					

Review the objectives for taking risks outlined earlier, noting which of your values are involved when you take the risk. Remember to ask not only what you could lose but what you could gain. Also, learn from the risks you have taken in the past. Build upon the successes you've already had.

For example, Ruby, an assistant manager in a branch of a large bank, has developed a new procedure to streamline customers' service. The procedure, however, requires the reassignment of some personnel and an initial financial investment by the bank. Presenting the procedure to her supervisors is a high risk for Ruby, since she has been on her current job for only six months, is the only black assistant manager in the bank (although there are black tellers), and does not know her supervisors very well. Yet her idea would provide a valuable service to the bank's customers and thus to the bank itself.

What can Ruby do to change this high risk into a moderate risk? First, she analyzes why her goal is so risky. She identifies her concerns— the fear that she will be perceived as a "pushy black broad who doesn't know what she is talking about" and the fear that her white male colleagues will be unresponsive to her ideas or take credit for them, as has occurred in the past. Ruby realizes that the risk appears high because she has been hurt in the past by such slights, not only at work but also in her personal life as part of growing up black and female. Yet she also realizes that it is possible to learn from these experiences and to move forward rather than becoming paralyzed.

Ruby next outlines what she could gain from taking the risk of presenting her plan. She recognizes that it would give her a chance (1) to participate in the implementation of the plan and thus learn more about the functions of the bank; (2) to enhance her prestige as a clear-thinking, intelligent employee concerned with the bank's interests; and (3) to express her creativity.

Ruby also lists what she could lose. She asks herself, "What is the worst thing that could happen?" Her response is, "I suppose they could fire me." Ruby realizes it is unlikely that her proposal would cause such an extreme reaction. Identifying and confronting this basic fear reduces her anxiety and thus the level of risk.

Ruby continues to review her goal, her concerns, the possible gains and losses, and develops several possible methods of introducing her plan. At this point, she asks two women she trusts to spend an hour with her brainstorming a list of possible activities and reviewing their feasibility. Although it is Ruby who will ultimately make the choice, her friends serve as soundingboards to help her clarify her thinking.

In the end, Ruby decides to spend an additional two months becoming more familiar with her work environment. She will seek opportunities to learn more about the bank's philosophy and policies, attend meetings where current problems are discussed, and talk with others at the bank who have the expertise she lacks. In other words, she plans to learn all she can about the "world" in which she works. Ruby will then rewrite her plan, incorporating her individual goal into the goals and needs of her bank. The extra time gives her the edge she needs to develop a convincing case.

In addition, Ruby decides to build an alliance with her boss and to find opportunities to enhance her boss's self-concept as she moves ahead on what she wants to do. Not viewing him as an enemy enables her to learn from his extensive experience. She decides that both they and the bank would benefit from a more collaborative relationship.

During this process, Ruby realizes that there will be setbacks, that some activities will not work on the first try, that new circumstances may raise new problems. Therefore, she and her two friends agree to meet every other week for lunch to review her progress. This lunch is an ongoing strategy session that provides her with a built-in support system to check on her progress and make suggestions if change is necessary.

Ruby has done it. She has taken what at first appeared to be an impossible dream and made it into a reality. The risk is now at a level she can effectively handle.

What about you?

Think about high risks you have taken that, upon reflection, could have been reduced to a moderate level through similar careful analysis and planning.

Here is a chance for you to develop a plan for taking a risk you currently face or anticipate facing in the near future. On the risk-taking worksheet (#45), list several risks and select one you'd like to take. Answer the questions and write down your plan of action. Describe the support you will seek to make your plan successful. Whether you focus on a risk in your personal life or your professional life, the idea is to plan. Planning is an integral part of risk taking; it organizes the process into manageable steps and thus reduces your anxiety and increases your willingness to continue taking rational, appropriate risks.

Your Personal Resources: Money, Time, and Health

In addition to the positive self-concept and healthy attitude toward risk, you have three valuable personal resources to assist you in achieving your goal: time, health, and money. The following checklists will help you assess how you stand.

---

45   PLAN FOR TAKING A RISK

List risks that you are either currently facing or anticipate facing in the near future:

1. _____

2. _____

3. _____

Select a risk you'd like to take and answer these questions:

1. What is the risk? What level of risk is it?

2. What do you want the results to be?

3. What concerns do you have about taking this risk?

4. What will you gain if you take this risk?

5. What will you lose if you take this risk?

6. How can you minimize any possible losses?

7. What options do you have in taking this risk?

8. How can you move the risk from a high level to a moderate level?

Plan of action

Support

Money

What money will you need to achieve your goal? Will you need money for additional professional development—for school tuition, books, or workshops? Will there be a loss of income while you prepare yourself professionally? How much money are you willing to invest in your future? What sources of money do you have (scholarships, loans, savings accounts, property)?

Time

Assess how much time you will need to pursue your career or prepare yourself for a selected leadership role. Make a list of the various activities that currently take up your time (work, family, personal interests, study). How can you adjust the total amount of time for each in order to pursue your goal? For example, if you decide to take six hours of credit at a local college, you need to take that time from another activity.

If you adjust the use of your time, what problems might arise and how can you solve them? If you take time from your home life, how will it affect family relationships? How will routine homemaking chores be done?

Health

Assess the condition of your health. Is it fair, good, excellent? What is your level of energy? What are you currently doing to maintain good physical health? What possible strains on your health might occur if you pursue your goal? How can you plan to ensure good health *and* pursue your goal?

Your Other Resources: People and Organizations

What people or groups make up your sources of support right now? What kinds of support do they give you? How satisfactory are these sources? Who else can help you reach your goal? What do they know that you need to know? Do you have a mentor? The support you get from other people is vital. While the kind and source of support may change with circumstance and age, the need is always there.

Marcille Gray Williams in *The New Executive Woman* takes an opposite position.[3] She believes the woman who reaches the executive suite has done it alone, through work and persistence, not collectivism. It is true that each woman must look out for herself; however, upward mobility is not achieved in isolation or without support from others. Even men who make it to top management positions have not done it alone. They were helped by the "old boy network," mentors, and other connections.

If, then, support is necessary, how much is reasonable? Because women tend to seek approval from others and to depend heavily on others for emotional and financial support, they do not learn to rely on their own intelligence, abilities, and strengths. The goal is to balance support and challenge. At times, of course, one is needed more than the other, and the balance is temporarily upset. Poor health, emotional vulnerability, personal or professional crises, or inadequate financial resources demand that you seek additional support *for the moment*. As circumstances improve, you lean toward challenging opportunities and activities.

What is important is that you determine what support you need and where you can get it and accept the need for support as a reality. Only you know what you need; others have only clues. You can best determine the correct proportion of support and challenge.

Figure 12. The intimacy scale.

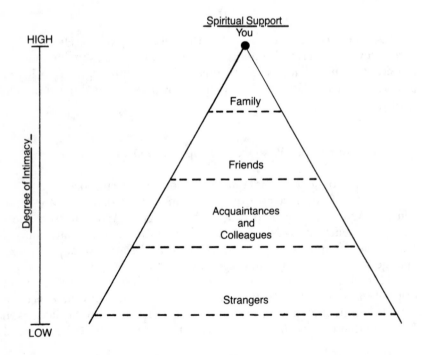

Support comes from many sources. These can be identified on a scale of intimacy, as shown in Figure 12. You are located at the pivotal point on the diagram. Above you, or beyond the human element, are your sources of spiritual support. While this support transcends human experience, it can also be a sustaining element in your survival. Below you are sources of human support, ranging from high to low in degree of intimacy. The widening lines indicate the number of people in each support group: There are fewer at the high end and more at the low end of the scale.

Friends, acquaintances, colleagues, and strangers offer a variety of support systems. These include mentorships, personal support groups, and professional organizations and associations. As you read about these sources below, keep in mind the kind of support you need to achieve your goal. Recall times when you needed support from a certain source and did or did not receive it.

Mentors

What is a mentor? Do you have one? Do you need one? How do you get one? The subject of mentors has gained prominence as women interested in managerial positions have found female models and sponsors to help them in their chosen path. Hennig and Jardim[4] and Gail Sheehy[5] have illustrated how instrumental mentors have been in the careers of successful women. A mentor can be an important source of support to any woman interested in leadership.

Mentor was a friend to whom Odysseus, when he was setting out for Troy, entrusted his house and the education of his son. From this story has emerged the meaning of mentor: a faithful counselor. Men have always had mentors, though they may not have recognized or called them as such. Usually, the mentor was 10 to 20 years older, wiser in the ways of the world, but interested in the same field as the younger person. Although mentors may not consciously recognize it, they often select a younger person who reminds them of themselves in their youth or who holds similar dreams. They may not really view the younger person as their child, yet in many ways they adopt a parental role.

What are the benefits of mentorship? The mentor is a "door opener," a conveyer of useful information, an encourager. The mentor may inspire the younger person to greater heights and suggest ways to attain her or his goals. The benefits appear one-sided, but the relationship is also rewarding to the mentor, who experiences the joy of teaching, leading, and watching an individual develop and of recognizing her or his talents. In addition, mentors gain satisfaction in continuing the tradition of helping others as they were helped early in their careers.

How does a mentorship relationship work? The following example is typical. Ann, a woman in her early thirties, had returned to graduate school for an advanced degree. One of her professors, Sid, recognized her intelligence, ability to organize, and creativity. Since she needed a part-time job, she began to work for Sid, helping him to organize his office and to coordinate many of his training programs. During the course of this working relationship, Sid often explored new ideas with Ann, encouraging her to express her opinions. He frequently gave her advice about useful courses to take, people to meet, and other experiences that would enhance her professional preparation. At times, he even counseled her about difficulties she was facing. Within six months, he asked her to take on more responsibilities, ones he was confident she could handle even though she wasn't so sure. Eventually, he even passed along consulting work for her that he was unable to fit into his schedule. Sid was clearly Ann's mentor, even though neither ever used the word. He recognized her potential, took extra time to help her grow, and in turn received the satisfaction of seeing the results of this nurturing process.

Problems, however, can also occur. As Sheehy notes in her studies, difficulty often arises when the protégé outgrows the mentor. At this point, the younger person may ridicule or forget the mentor or worship from a distance. Although many mentorships evolve into friendships, it is not always easy to terminate the relationship on a positive note.

Another problem cited by Sheehy is that a sexual relationship may develop between an older male mentor and a younger career woman. The closeness and frequent interaction between the two can easily lead to a physical relationship. While this can initially be satisfactory, it frequently complicates the mentor relationship and usually ends with the woman shut out from the personal intimacy and professional contact that originally drew her to the mentor.

A third problem is that the male mentor and his female protégé often differ in their perceptions of each other's role. In this case, Sheehy says, the mentor gets more than he bargained for. The female enters the relationship seeking his approval and wanting him to cherish her both personally and professionally—that is, to be a surrogate parent. When he doesn't meet these needs—which he was never aware of—she is hurt. A male protégé, on the other hand, generally expects less from the relationship. Also, men usually have less difficulty understanding each other's needs.

FINDING A MENTOR

Traditionally, mentorships seem to "just happen." They develop informally between people who have a professional relationship and who would probably not openly acknowledge it as a mentorship.

However, if women want to successfully move into responsible leadership positions, they can't afford to let things "just happen"; they need to *make* things happen. Also, they needn't suffer from some of the problems that often plague others involved in mentorships. The following is a concrete, non-traditional method to help you find, use, and prosper from a mentor.

How do you know if you need a mentor? Consider the following questions:

Are you relatively new to your profession or field? Would you benefit from working with someone who has had more years of experience? Do you lack access to people and other resources that would help you achieve your goal? If you would benefit from a mentor, follow the steps outlined below to make sure you establish a successful and healthy relationship.

First, decide what a mentor would provide for you. What do you need that you cannot get from other sources? Develop criteria for a mentor. Think about what you specifically want from the other person. For example: How much time would you expect from the mentor? How dependent do you want to be? Is a sexual relationship ruled out completely or a possibility? Does it matter whether your mentor is a man or a woman?

Next identify possible mentors. Look in your organization and your profession. Ask others for recommendations. Make a list of prospects, apply your criteria, and rank them accordingly. Interview each prospect. Be assertive. Call and arrange to talk. Tell each one you are seeking a mentor. Most will probably be both surprised and flattered, as they have undoubtedly never been interviewed to be a mentor. Once you have interviewed everyone, select the mentor who best suits your needs. As in any important relationship, you may not find a person who meets all your qualifications, but you can get the best possible match.

Make an agreement with your mentor. Discuss and put into writing the following:

—What you want from the relationship (resources, contacts, "door opening," counseling).
—What the mentor wants from you in return (loyalty, specific skills, free labor).
—Approximate length of time for the relationship. If this cannot be determined now, set a date for reviewing the relationship to decide if it should be continued.
—Your commitment, as protégé, to someday become a mentor, preferably to another woman.

The commitment to assume the role of a mentor at a later date, especially to other women, is of particular importance. Part of the difficulty women have in moving up into leadership positions is that they lack role models and mentors. As women achieve new heights, they have a responsibility to reach out to women behind them and offer assistance. Do not let your own difficulty in reaching your goal be an excuse for failing to make someone else's advancement easier.

The commitment to become a mentor makes it easier for the protégé to ask for support, knowing that she will later provide similar assistance to another. It also reassures her mentor that this relationship will be temporary and is one in a long chain of support.

Monitor your relationship and your growth carefully, regularly, and honestly. If the relationship is not giving you what you want and attempts to correct it haven't helped, find a new mentor. You are, after all, not obligated for life. As your needs change, move toward more independence. Remember, you agreed that the mentorship would be temporary and would continue only as long as each of you benefited. You needn't feel guilty for moving on, but do reassure your mentor of her or his worth to you.

Leave when you are ready. At some point you will find you no longer need a mentor. How will you know? Your feelings of self-confidence will be strong and consistent, and you will not need to rely as much on others for ideas and advice. When you are ready, go!

Finally, open yourself to the role of mentor. Look for people in need of a mentor and pass along the support. Teach your protégé the process and grow together.

Personal support groups

Personal support groups may be comprised of acquaintances, colleagues, or even strangers. They include women's consciousness-raising groups (CR) and personal growth workshops (human relations courses, couples workshops, encounter groups). Techniques such as values clarification, transactional analysis (TA), reality therapy, re-evaluation counseling, transcendental meditation (TM), and Gestalt therapy are used to achieve the goals of the group.

With the recent popularity of self-help groups, you should have little difficulty finding a personal support group that fits your needs. In addition, many self-help books are available to help you get in touch with your potential, your feelings, and your strengths (see the resources section).

What are the benefits of personal support groups? For many women, the primary benefit is self-validation. As women move into the "foreign" territory of leadership, they may experience many doubts, fears, and anxieties. Sharing these feelings with others can reduce their isolation ("You mean you feel that way too?") and give them encouragement that they are on the right track ("We know you can do it!"). These groups can be invaluable sources of personal validation and can offer additional resources to assist you in your plan of action.

If you cannot find a group that meets your needs, you may want to form a group of your own. First decide what you need that available sources of support can't supply. Think of other people who might want to become involved in such a group. Explain your ideas about the group and listen to their ideas.

Hold an organizing meeting with interested people. Review the needs of each person, reach a consensus on the group's purpose, meeting time, location, and procedures, and determine the resources needed (money, materials, room). After the group is established, periodically review the original purpose and procedures to ensure that people's needs are still being met.

When you no longer need the support of the group, move on. As in mentorship, this source of support, although important, is temporary. Continuously assess the kind of support you need.

Professional support groups

Professional support groups consist of professionals with a common interest who seek development in their field. Personal development occurs indirectly, but the primary goal is professional growth. Members meet periodically to learn from each other, share resources useful to their profession, and support each other's efforts. Examples include support groups made up of teachers from a certain grade level, high school department heads, women administrators in higher education, women graduate students of business, women artists or writers, and women personnel officers.

The professional support group may provide many of the same services offered by a professional organization or association. Generally, however, the support group is smaller and more focused, meets more frequently, and offers greater opportunities for social and emotional interaction.

The professional support group can be a place to exchange ideas related to your profession; to get practical help from others in problem solving or other skills; and to test out a new skill or idea before risking it in the "real" world. Like the personal support group, it can reduce the isolation many women experience as they move up and offer an opportunity to share pains and disappointments as well as accomplishments. It can be a time of rejuvenation that gives you the extra energy and motivation you need.

If you want to start a professional support group of your own, read Kirschenbaum and Glaser's *Developing Support Groups: A Manual for Facilitators and Participants.* Among other topics, it outlines what to consider when you select others for the group (how much the members should have in common), the optimal size (8 to 12 people), and specific procedures for group meetings.

Professional organizations and associations

Professional organizations are usually more formally organized and more enduring than professional support groups. Membership may be local, regional, national, and even international. Members may include men, women, or both. These groups are organized around a common interest, such as education, politics, or social service. Some may be organized around a more specialized interest, such as gender, race, or religion.

How can you find a professional organization or association suited to your needs? Review what is available. A list of professional women's groups is given at the end of this book. Many of these organizations may be a source of support for you right now.

Become more familiar with the organizations that interest you. Ask other women who belong to professional associations about their experiences. Attend a meeting of each organization that interests you. If there is more than one chapter of an organization in your area, visit them all, since their focus and activities may differ.

Join the group or groups that best meet your needs. And, as before, when you no longer need the support, move on.

Planning for support

At this point, you should have a clearer idea of the sources of support that can help you become an effective leader. List your specific needs in seeking support and potential sources in chart **#46.** Then determine the steps you must take to obtain the support. Incorporate this information into your plan of action at the end of the chapter.

Planning for Action—Now

By this time you have gathered enough information about your risk-taking style, resources, sources of support, and environment to develop a short-term plan of action that will move you closer to your long-term career goal.

46 SOURCES OF SUPPORT

Need	Source of support: personal contact, mentor, personal support group, professional support group, professional organization	Currently available (Yes/No)	Steps to obtain support

Tips for planning

Here are some tips to help you in developing a plan.

Break it up. Looking at a problem as a whole can be discouraging and overwhelming. Many people give up shortly after making a New Year's resolution because they have not broken the problem into manageable parts. For example, Delia's resolution to say no to requests from others may work for a day or a week, but she will most likely slip into her old pattern of saying yes unless she breaks up desired behavior change into manageable parts. To begin with, Delia can log all the requests made of her for three days and decide to say no to those requiring the least risk, such as requests from salespeople or acquaintances on committees. After she has succeeded with this step, she can move on to requests carrying higher risk, such as those made by her family and close friends. She continues in this fashion until she has achieved her goal. This step-by-step process breaks the problem into manageable parts and increases her likelihood of success.

Be flexible. Military plans and football tactics are not set in stone, nor should your plans be. Expect the need for change and adaptation. When it arises, don't become immobilized: Do something. If one strategy doesn't work, modify or drop it and think of another. For example, if the strategy described above isn't working, Delia "goes back to the drawing board," reviews the kinds of requests made of her, and explores why she has such trouble saying no. She may seek out counseling to explore the problem.

Use it, don't file it. Once you have developed your plan, use it. It is of no use to you in your drawer of file. Carry a copy of your plan with you to review as the occasion arises. Post a copy where you can see it daily so that your goals receive primary attention and you develop daily activities to help you accomplish them. Write down your current short-term goal on an index card and carry it with you. For example, Delia currently carries a small card that reads: "What will I gain and what will I lose if I say no to this request?" Whenever she receives a request by phone or in person, she asks herself this question. She leaves the card by her phone at home and on her desk at work as a reminder. Eventually she will automatically ask herself this question and no longer need the card as her aid.

Four-step planning

Four steps are involved in developing a final plan: (1) restate your goal; (2) develop strategies to reach your goal; (3) determine activities to achieve each strategy; and (4) prepare a time action chart.

RESTATE YOUR GOAL

Once again, review the goal statement you previously wrote. Make any necessary changes. Prepare a final statement before you proceed. For example, Barbara, who has worked in education, decides that she wants a middle management position in a profit-making organization within five years. She wants to work in a small or medium-size business in the field of communications that will give her the opportunity to assume increasingly responsible roles. She is willing to live anywhere in the United States.

DEVELOP STRATEGIES

A strategy is a method for achieving a goal. Using the strategy worksheet (#47), list as many strategies as you can think of to help you achieve your goal. Be general at this point; you will identify more specific activities in the next step. The strategies do not need to be in any particular order. Then identify the helping or hindering forces (skills, attitudes, money, health, past experience) affecting each strategy.

For example, Barbara assesses her skills, interests, and needs, and lists four strategies to accomplish her stated goal: (1) obtaining an MBA degree, (2) finding a mentor, (3) gaining experience in a profit-making organization, and (4) doing research on organizational behavior. For obtaining an MBA degree, she lists the following forces:

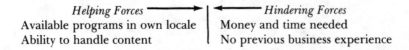

Helping Forces ———→	←——— *Hindering Forces*
Available programs in own locale	Money and time needed
Ability to handle content	No previous business experience

Finally, rank the strategies according to their ability to help you reach your goal, with 1 representing the best strategy, 2 the next best, and so forth.

DETERMINE YOUR ACTIVITIES

An activity is a specific procedure for carrying out a strategy. You are now ready to be more specific about the activities needed to achieve your goal.

Barbara, having decided on obtaining an MBA as her primary strategy, lists the following activities:

Request a leave of absence from my school district.
Review colleges of business administration in my state.
Apply to three graduate programs.
Ask for recommendations from four colleagues.

Possible strategies	Helping forces	Hindering forces	Ranking
1.			
2.			
3.			
4.			

48   ACTIVITY SHEET

Strategy 1: _____

    Activities

        1.

        2.

        3.

        4.

        5.

Strategy 2: _____

    Activities

        1.

        2.

        3.

        4.

        5.

Strategy 3: _____

    Activities

        1.

        2.

        3.

        4.

        5.

Strategy 4: _____

    Activities

        1.

        2.

        3.

        4.

        5.

Goal: A position in middle management in a profit-making organization

Activities	Others involved	1979										1980								
		Mar	Apr	May	June	July	Aug	Sept	Oct	Nov	Dec	Jan	Feb	Mar	Apr	May	June	July	Aug	Sept
Review possible graduate business programs																				
Apply to three schools																				
Ask for recommendations	Professors																			
Request leave of absence																				
Read *Managerial Woman*																				
Read *Passages* on mentors																				
Rewrite vitae																				
Review employment opportunities near schools																				
Once accepted, prepare list of businesses to apply to for work																				
Set up appointments for job interviews																				
Take a vacation																				
Identify some people in field of interest to interview																				
Find a place to live																				
Prepare for move and move																				
Set up interviews with contacts																				

Goal:

Activities	Others involved	Dates																			

Using chart **#48,** prepare your own list of activities for each of the important strategies you have selected. It is helpful to brainstorm at this point—that is, to write down everything that occurs to you. Do not evaluate any item until you've exhausted the possibilities. Ask other people to suggest activities you might consider. Remember, however, that you know best. Only you can decide which strategies and activities will best serve you. Information from other sources may help you make up your mind, but you must determine your own plan.

Prepare a Time Action Chart

You are now ready to develop a formal "game plan"—and plan for *now.* Your objective in this final step is to develop a schedule of activities for achieving your goal and to lay them out on a time action chart. Barbara's time action chart **(#49)** illustrates her final plan. Note that the plan focuses on her primary strategy of obtaining an MBA degree, but also includes activities related to her secondary strategies.

Look at your list of strategies and activities. Identify which can be started immediately and which can be started in one month, six months, and so forth. Assign each activity an estimated date or month. Transfer each activity onto your personal time action chart **(#50),** listing each in the order needed to carry out your plan. List months across the top of the chart. Draw a line from the date you will start each activity to the date you will (or must) finish. Indicate others who might be involved in accomplishing each activity.

Conclusion

You now have everything you need to start on your plan—today. You have explored what you want, its costs and rewards, and the knowledge and skills you have and will need to be an effective leader. You have also developed a time action chart of activities that will lead you to achieving your goal.

You've got your roadmap, so get started!

REFERENCES

1. Sidney Simon, *I Am Loveable and Capable* (Niles, IL: Argus Communications, 1973).
2. Margaret Hennig and Anne Jardim, *The Managerial Woman* (New York: Doubleday, 1977), pp. 27-29.
3. Marcille Gray Williams, *The New Executive Woman* (Radnor, PA: Chilton Book Company, 1977).
4. Hennig and Jardim, *Managerial Woman,* pp. 123-154.

5. Gail Sheehy, "The Mentor's Connection—The Secret Link in the Successful Woman's Life," *New York,* April 5, 1978, pp. 33-38.

RESOURCES

Personal Development

Alberti, Robert, and Michael Emmons. *Your Perfect Right.* San Luis Obispo, CA: Impact, 1977.

Bloom, Lunn, Karen Cobur, and Joan Pearlman. *The New Assertive Woman.* New York: Dell, 1975.

Canfield, Jack, and H. Wells. *100 Ways to Build Self-Concept in the Classroom.* La Jolla, CA: University Associates.

Harris, Thomas. *I'm OK, You're OK.* New York: Harper & Row, 1967.

Howe, Leland. *Taking Charge of Your Life,* 1977. Available from National Humanistic Education Center, 110 Spring Street, Saratoga Springs, NY 12866.

James, Muriel, and Dorothy Jongeward. *Born to Win.* Reading, MA: Addison-Wesley, 1971.

Simon, Sidney. *I Am Loveable and Capable.* Niles, IL: Argus Communications, 1973.

Simon, Sidney. *Meeting Yourself Halfway.* Niles, IL: Argus Communications, 1976.

Getting Support from Others

Chesler, Phyllis. "Are We a Threat to Each Other?" *MS,* October 1972, p. 86.

Hennig, Margaret, and Anne Jardim. *The Managerial Woman.* New York: Doubleday, 1977.

Kirschenbaum, Howard, and Barbara Glaser. *Developing Support Groups: A Manual for Facilitators and Participants.* La Jolla, CA: University Associates, 1978.

Sheehy, Gail. "The Mentor's Connection—The Secret Link in the Successful Woman's Life." *New York,* April 5, 1978, pp. 33-38.

Planning for Action

Bolles, Richard Nelson. *What Color Is Your Parachute? A Practical Manual for Job Hunters and Career Changers.* Berkeley, CA: Ten Speed Press, 1978.

Scholz, Nelle, Judith Prince, and Gordon Miller. *How to Decide—A Guide for Women.* New York: College Entrance Examination Board, 1975.

PROFESSIONAL WOMEN'S GROUPS*

Academy of Management
Committee on the Status of Women
in the Management Profession
2700 Bay Area Blvd.
Houston, TX 77058

Adult Education Association of the
USA
Commission on the Status of Women
810 18th St., NW, Suite 500
Washington, D.C. 20006

*This listing is adapted from one developed in May 1978 by the American Association of University Women (AAUW), 2401 Virginia Avenue, NW, Washington, D.C., 20037, and the Project on the Status and Education of Women, Association of American Colleges, 1818 R Street, NW, Washington, D.C., 20009.

American Academy of Religion
Women's Caucus—Religious Studies
Department of Religion, Douglass
College
Rutgers University
New Brunswick, NJ 08903

American Alliance for Health,
Physical Education and Recreation
Task Force on Equal Opportunity
and Human Rights
1201 16th St., NW
Washington, D.C. 20036

American Anthropological
Association
Committee on the Status of Women
in Anthropology
1703 New Hampshire Ave., NW
Washington, D.C. 20009

American Association for Higher
Education
Women's Caucus
One Dupont Circle
Washington, D.C. 20036

American Association for the
Advancement of Science
Office of Opportunities in Science
1776 Massachusetts Avenue, NW
Washington, D.C. 20036

American Association of
Immunologists
Women and Minority Group
Immunologists
9650 Rockville Pike
Bethesda, MD 20014

American Association of University
Professors
Committee on the Status of Women
in the Academic Profession
One Dupont Circle, Suite 500
Washington, D.C. 20036

American Association of Women in
Community and Junior Colleges
Center for Women's Opportunities
One Dupont Circle, NW, Suite 401/
AAC JC
Washington, D.C. 20036

American Chemical Society
Women Chemists Committee
1155 16th St., NW
Washington, D.C. 20036

American College Personnel
Association
(Division of APGA)
Women's Task Force
1607 New Hampshire Ave., NW
Washington, D.C. 20009

American Education Research
Association
Committee on Women in Education
Research
1126 16th St., NW
Washington, D.C. 20036

American Federation of Teachers
Human Rights and Community
Relations Dept.
Women's Rights Committee
11 Dupont Circle, NW
Washington, D.C. 20036

American Geological Institute
Women Geoscientists Committee
5205 Leesburg Pike
Falls Church, VA 22041

American Historical Association
Committee on Women Historians
400 A Street, SE
Washington, D.C. 20003

American Humanist Association
602 Third St.
San Francisco, CA 94107

American Institute of Chemists
Professional Opportunities for
Women Committee
7315 Wisconsin Ave.
Washington, D.C. 20014

American Institute of Planners
Women's Rights (Joint Committee
with the American Society of
Planning Officials)
1776 Massachusetts Ave., NW
Washington, D.C. 20036

American Library Association
Committee on Status of Women in
Librarianship
c/o Margaret Myers
50 E. Hurton St.
Chicago, IL 60611

American Medical Women's
Association, Inc.
1740 Broadway
New York, New York 10019

American Nurses Association
2420 Pershing Rd.
Kansas City, MO 64108

American Personnel and Guidance
Association
Women's Committee
1607 New Hampshire Ave., NW
Washington, D.C. 20009

American Philosophical Association
Committee on the Status of Women
Exec. Sec.: Mr. John O'Connor
U. of Delaware
Newark, DE 19711

American Physical Society
Committee on the Status of Women
in Physics
335 E. 45th St.
New York, NY 10017

American Political Science
Association
Committee on the Status of Women
in the Profession
1527 New Hampshire Ave., NW
Washington, D.C. 20036

American Psychiatric Association
Committee on Women
1700 18th St., NW
Washington, D.C. 20009

American Psychological Association
Committee on Women in Psychology
1200 17th St., NW
Washington, D.C. 20036

American Public Health Association,
Inc.

Standing Committee of Women's
Rights
Women's Caucus
1015 18th St., NW
Washington, D.C. 20036

American Society for Microbiology
Committee on the Status of Women
Microbiologists
1913 I St., NW
Washington, D.C. 20006

American Society for Public
Administration
Committee on Women in Public
Administration
1225 Connecticut Ave., NW, Suite
300
Washington, D.C. 20036

American Society for Training and
Development
Women's Caucus
One Dupont Circle, Suite 400
Washington, D.C. 20036

American Society of Biological
Chemists
Committee on Equal Opportunities
for Women
9650 Rockville Pike
Bethesda, MD 20014

American Society of Planning
Officials
Women's Rights Committee (See
American Institute of Planners)
1313 E. 60th St.
Chicago, IL 60637

American Sociological Association
Committee on the Status of Women
in Sociology
1722 N St., NW
Washington, D.C. 20036

American Speech and Hearing
Association
Committee on the Equality of the
Sexes
10801 Rockville Pike
Rockville, MD 20852

American Statistical Association
Women's Caucus
Committee on Women in Statistics
806 15th St., NW
Washington, D.C. 20005

American Studies Association
Women's Committee
4025 Chestnut St., T7
U. of Penn.
Philadelphia, PA 19104

American Women in Radio and
Television, Inc.
Affirmative Action Committee
1321 Connecticut Ave., NW
Washington, DC 20016

Association for Asian Studies
Committee on the Role of Women in
Asian Studies
One Lane Hall
U. of Michigan
Ann Arbor, MI 48109

Association for Women in
Mathematics
c/o Dept. of Mathematics
Mills College, Oakland, CA 94613

Association for Women in Psychology
c/o Dept. of Psychology
Southern Illinois University
Carbondale, IL 62901

Association for Women in Science
1346 Connecticut Ave., NW, No. 1122
Washington, D.C. 20036

Association of American
Geographers
Committee on the Status of Women
in Geography
1710 16th St., NW
Washington, D.C. 20006

Association of American Law Schools
Section of Women in Legal
Education
One Dupont Circle, NW
Washington, D.C. 20036

Association of American Women
Dentists
435 N. Michigan Ave., 17th Floor
Chicago, IL 60611

B'nai B'rith Women
1640 Rhode Island Ave., NW
Washington, D.C. 20036

Church Employed Women
475 Riverside Dr., Rm. 1260
New York, NY 10027

College Art Association of America
Committee on the Status of Women
in the Profession
16 E. 52 St.
New York, NY 10022

College Music Society
Committee on the Status of Women
Dept. of Music
State University of New York at
Binghamton
Binghamton, NY 13901

The Coordinating Committee on
Women in the Historical Profession—
Conference Group on Women's
History
c/o 6 N. Highland Pl.
Croton-on-Hudson, NY 10520

Federally Employed Women
National Press Bldg., No. 485
Washington, D.C. 20045

Federation of Organizations for
Professional Women
2000 P St., NW, No. 403
Washington, D.C. 20036

Feminist Law Students Association
U. of Santa Clara School of Law
Santa Clara, CA 95053

Latin American Studies Association
Committee on Women
c/o Johns Hopkins University
1740 Massachusetts Ave., NW
Washington, D.C. 20036

Linguistic Society of America
Committee on the Status of Women
in Linguistics
1161 N. Kent St.
Arlington, VA 22209

Modern Language Association
Commission on the Status of Women
in the Profession
62 Fifth Ave.
New York, NY 10011

National Association for Female
Executives
160 E. 65th St.
New York, NY 10022

National Association for Women
Deans, Administrators, and
Counselors
1028 Connecticut Ave., NW
Washington, D.C. 20036

National Association of Bank Women
111 E. Wacker Dr.
Chicago, IL 60601

National Association of Media
Women
157 W. 126 St.
New York, NY 10027

National Association of Social
Workers
National Committee on Women's
Issues
1425 H St., NW
Washington, DC 20005

National Association of Women
Lawyers
American Bar Center
1155 E. 60 St.
Chicago, IL 60637

The National Chamber of Commerce
for Women, Inc.
"Household Risk Management, Jobs,
and Business Service for Women"
Action Committee
1623 Connecticut Ave., NW
Washington, DC 20009

National Council for the Social
Studies
Advisory Committee on Sexism and
Social Justice
1515 Wilson Blvd.
Arlington, VA 22209

National Council of Administrative
Women in Education
1815 T. Meyer Dr. N.
Arlington, VA 22209

National Council of Teachers of
English
Women's Committee
1111 Kenyon Rd.
Urbana, IL 61801

National Council on Family Relations
Task Force on Women's Rights and
Responsibilities
c/o Department of Sociology
San Diego State U.
San Diego, CA. 92182

National Dental Association
734 15th St., NW, Suite 500
Washington, D.C. 20005

National Education Association
Women's Caucus
1201 16th St., NW
Washington, D.C. 20036

National Recreation and Park
Association
Office of Women's and Minority
Programs
1601 N. Kent St.
Arlington, VA 22209

National University Extension
Association
Division of Women's Education
Concerns of Women Committee
One Dupont Circle, Suite 360
Washington, D.C. 20036

Nuclear Energy Women
Energy Information
Duke Power Co.
P.O. Box 2178
Charlotte, NC 28242

Organization of American Historians
Committee on the Status of Women
in the Profession
112 N. Bryan St.
Bloomington, IN 47401

Population Association of America
Women's Caucus
P. O. Box 14182
Benjamin Franklin Station
Washington, D.C. 20044

Public Relations Society of America
845 Third Ave.
New York, NY 10022

Society for Women in Philosophy
2020 Willistead Crescent
Windsor, Ontario, Canada N86 IK5

220

Society of American Archivists
Committee on the Status of Women
in the Archival Profession
P.O. Box 8198
UICC Library
Chicago, IL 60680

Society of Women Engineers
United Engineering Center
Rm. 305
345 E. 47 St.
New York, NY 10017

Sociologists for Women in Society
P. O. Box 751
Portland State U.
Portland, OR 97207

Speech Communication Association
Women's Caucus
5202 Leesburg Pike
Falls Church, VA 22041

United Presbyterian Church in the
USA
Council on Women and the Church
475 Riverside Dr.
New York, NY 10027

Women Educators
P. O. Box 218
Red Bank, NJ 07701

Women in Architecture, Landscape
Architecture, and Planning
Boston Architectural Center
320 Newberry St.
Boston, MA 02115

Women in Communications, Inc.
P. O. Box 9561
Austin, TX 78766

Women in Science and Engineering
c/o Dr. Miriam Schweber
22 Turning Mill Rd.
Lexington, MA 02173

Women's Caucus for Art
Affirmative Action Committee
Dept. of Art and Art History
U. of Missouri-Kansas City
Kansas City, MO 64110

Women's Caucus for Political Science
Mt. Vernon College
2100 Foxhall Rd.
Washington, D.C. 20007

Women's Caucus for the Modern
Languages
Univ. of Wisconsin
Milwaukee, WI 53201

Women's Classical Caucus
Hunter College
Box 126A
695 Park Ave.
New York, NY 10021

Women's Veterinary Medical
Association
29500 Heathercliff Rd.
Malibu, CA 90265

Women Working in Construction
1854 Wyoming Ave., NW
Washington, D.C. 20009

Index